Cranmer
in Context

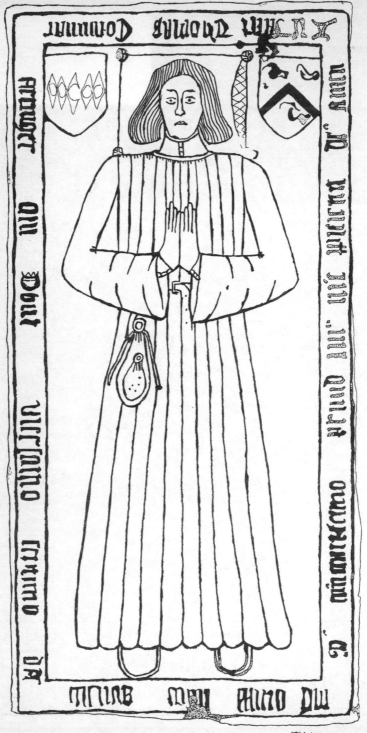

J. Wallace.

Cranmer in Context

Peter Newman Brooks

Ⓛ

Lutterworth Press
Cambridge

Dedication

Hunc libellum discipulis suis tam Erasmi quam Lutheri fautoribus,
quos per plures quam meminisse juvat annos edocuit,
grato amicissimoque animo dedicat auctor.

Lutterworth Press
P.O. Box 60
Cambridge CB1 2NT

British Library Cataloguing in Publication Data
Brooks, Peter Newman, 1931 -
   Cranmer in context.
   1. Church of England, Cranmer, Thomas, 1489 - 1556
   I. Title
   283'. 09'4

ISBN 0-7188-2790-2

First published 1989 by Lutterworth Press

Printed in Great Britain by
The Guernsey Press Co. Ltd, Guernsey, Channel Islands

Contents

List of Illustrations

*The frontispiece is the work of John Graham Wallace, and is an exact sketch of the life-size memorial stone to Thomas Cranmer's father, now set in the floor of a chapel dedicated to Thomas Cranmer at Whatton Church, Nottinghamshire. It depicts a squire in repose, at prayer, his head resting upon a cushion set between the family arms. The right-hand shield is of particular interest, showing a Chevron and three Cranes: a heraldic pun for *Crane Mere*. The lake that provided a habitat for these fine birds gave its name to the Cranmer family village, Aslockton.

The debased Gothic inscription reads:
> Hic iacet Thomas Cornmar [sic]
> armiger qui obiit vicesimo septimo die
> mensis maii anno Dmi
> D millesimo
> M quincen primo cuius anime propicietur Deus Amen

(Here lies Thomas Cranmer, Gentleman, who died on the 27th day of the month of May in the year of the Lord 1501: May God have mercy on his soul. Amen.)

Preface

Cranmer in Context is a book of edited extracts from the writings of the Tudor primate who was born five hundred years ago, on 2 July 1489. His writings were once readily available, but are now hard to find. In 1833, under the somewhat morbid title *Remains of Thomas Cranmer, D.D.*, the Oxford University Press published a fine collection of the archbishop's work, and in 1846 John Edmund Cox edited most of Cranmer for the Parker Society. Nowadays, by contrast, it is difficult to obtain Cranmer material, even in worship. Indeed, since the publication of the *Alternative Service Book* in 1980, the 1662 revision of Cranmer's incomparable liturgy has increasingly disappeared from English parish churches where it has been replaced, almost as a matter of policy, by the cumbrous new rites that comprise the *ASB* (*'Anglican' Service Book* surely, as clergy seem rarely to recognise its rightful use as a properly accredited *Alternative*).

A quincentenary celebration ought certainly to prompt a wider public to examine at least something of Cranmer's legacy; and this volume is published to set the spotlight on the remarkable contribution he made to sixteenth-century national politics and piety. By reason of its transient appeal, commemorative material can be slick and unsustained. It can too be almost non-existent. Strange to state, the German Democratic Republic did more for Luther (despite the Peasants' Revolt, 1525), and the English Methodists more for John Wesley, than the English Establishment, whether ecclesiastical or cultural, has planned for Cranmer.

In fact, as an archbishop of the Reformation, Thomas Cranmer was one of those who moulded the English Church when Henry VIII's vision of 'imperial kingship' and independence determined on schism with Rome. Cranmer then had the task of presiding over a Church in transition - revising services, re-formulating doctrine, and re-drafting law. In pastoral ministry he afforded both faithful and not-so-faithful reasonable diversity of worship within a single comprehensive Church. Cranmer was grounded in the new Erasmian divinity at Cambridge, and his ambassadorial service and contact with the Lutheran centre of Nürnberg considerably widened his original expertise. Yet despite considerable intellectual development, a life-time's study of scripture and of his beloved 'old authors' (a term he used for the early Fathers of the Church), and the burdensome existence of the Tudor Court, he retained much of the characteristic moderation that makes him of real significance for English people and English-speaking culture. Even in his most 'Protestant' period, moreover, Cranmer remained very much an Erasmian in his avoidance of extremes. Such charitable supposition in trying times certainly made good political sense, and in addition held real pastoral potential.

Hans Holbein did not paint Cranmer, but the portrait painted by Flicke in July 1546, now in the Tudor room of the National Portrait Gallery in London, superbly depicts the scholar who, though once a remote, even ineffectual, Cambridge don, was to make a massive contribution to his times. The portrait also provides a valuable visual insight into the man, for on his desk may be seen not merely a work of St Augustine, and the influential edition of the Greek and Latin New Testament collated by Erasmus, but also a communication from the royal Council addressed to Cranmer as *Lorde tharbusshope of Canterbury*. He may well be reading the letters of Paul the apostle, but Cranmer's robes and ring project an image of him not as a narrow-minded churchman but rather as a notable ecclesiastical statesman. Like his portrait, these pages provide an introduction to the life and work of a significant scholar-priest. His active ministry in high places sets him in the front rank of reform in Tudor England, just as the liturgical grasp that composed the *Books of Common Prayer* (1549 and 1552) earns its author a literary reputation that is well-nigh Shakespearean. High claims perhaps, but readily substantiated in this book, particularly in the wide range of extracts it contains from the correspondence, controversies, treatises and prayers of the sensitive soul whose genius made enduring virtue from temporary compromise.

Dedicated with much affection to past and present pupils, too numerous to name, this book has also been specially written for the general reader who, at this time of commemoration, would like to know more of Cranmer through his own words. Particular appreciation must also be recorded to a select few for their counsel and support: Richard Sumner, who personifies principle and practice; to

Gregory Cameron, learned in law and gospel; to Matthew Dickens, sensitive scholar and sacristan; to John Graham Wallace, for his fine etching of the memorial stone to Cranmer's father, reproduced here by permission of the vicar, wardens, and council of the Cranmer group of parishes, diocese of Southwell; to Mrs Alison Houghton, librarian of Robinson College, Cambridge, for innumerable kindnesses; to Dr John Chadwick FBA, for classical expertise and true friendship through many a crisis; to Paul Ayris, my former PhD student, who shares the subject interest; to David Miller, a colourful Erasmian of acute mind; to Thomas Brinsley Hayward, a prying and persuasive little pixie without whose constant attention this work would have been finished in half the time; and especially to my long-suffering family, who have born the burden even a little volume brings to those obliged to deal with an author's obsession.

Peter Newman Brooks

Landbeach,
Easter Day 1989

List of Abbreviations

A & M: The Acts and Monuments of John Foxe, edited in eight volumes by J. Pratt (London, 1877).

A R G: Archiv für Reformationsgeschichte

Burnet: The History of the Reformation of the Church of England, by G. Burnet, edited in seven volumes by N. Pocock (Oxford, 1865).

Censura: Censura Martini Buceri, edited by E.C. Whitaker for the Alcuin Club (1974).

Cranmer I: Writings and Disputations of Thomas Cranmer, Archbishop of Canterbury, Martyr, 1556, Relative to the Sacrament of the Lord's Supper, edited by J.E. Cox, for the Parker Society (Cambridge, 1844).

Cranmer II: Miscellaneous Writings and Letters of Thomas Cranmer, Archbishop of Canterbury, Martyr, 1556, edited by J.E. Cox, for the Parker Society (Cambridge, 1846).

J E H: Journal of Ecclesiastical History

L & P: Calendar of Letters and Papers, Foreign and Domestic, of the Reign of Henry VIII, edited by J.S. Brewer, J. Gairdner and R.H. Brodie, in twenty-one volumes (London, 1862-1910).

L W: Luther's Works, edited by J. Pelikan and H.T. Lehmann, in fifty-five volumes (St Louis and Philadelphia, 1957-86).

Narratives: Narratives of the Days of the Reformation, edited by J.G. Nichols for the Camden Society (London, 1859).

Liturgies of Edward VI: The Two Liturgies A.D. 1549, and A.D. 1552: with other documents set forth by authority in the reign of Edward VI, edited by J. Ketley, for the Parker Society (Cambridge, 1844).

Original Letters: Original Letters relative to the English Reformation written during the reigns of Henry VIII, King Edward VI and Queen Mary: chiefly from the Archives of Zürich, edited by H. Robinson, in two volumes, for the Parker Society (Cambridge, 1846-7).

Ridley: The Works of Nicholas Ridley, D.D., sometime Lord Bishop of London, Martyr, 1555, edited by Henry Christmas, for the Parker Society, (Cambridge, 1843).

Please note that original source material illustrating the narrative appears at the end of each chapter.

There are no footnotes to burden the text, for most of the sources are well known. Works referred to are to be found listed in the Bibliography.

1
The Renaissance World of Learning

Cranmer was educated at a time of change and transition. He probably faced *antiqua severitas* and intimidation by rote learning, almost certainly followed by attendance at a grammar school to provide the link with Cambridge, where the boy was sent at 14 years of age [**Extract 1**]. Entering a new and undistinguished society (Jesus College had been founded from a convent of Benedictine nuns in 1496), young Thomas, according to a reminiscence of Morice, his secretary and first biographer, 'was nosseled in the grossest kynd of sophistry', being obliged to familiarise himself with that *sine qua non* of the Schools, *trivium* and *quadrivium*. The former embraced Latin grammar, an ABC range of rhetoric (Aristotle, Boethius and Cicero), with, of course, logic; and the latter arithmetic, geometry, music and astronomy.

Proceeding to the BA in 1511, Cranmer gained with the degree his first real opportunity for theological study, not that a college with statutes specifically framed to cut the canon law down to size allowed a junior fellow to elect otherwise. So at this stage (1511-14), Magister Cranmer absorbed what he regarded as the obscurities of scholastic philosophy [**Extract 2**]. It should be recalled that 1511 was the year in which the great Erasmus accepted Fisher's invitation to lecture at Cambridge; and as reader to the Lady Margaret, Europe's most distinguished classical scholar held forth on basic Greek grammar for a single hour every weekday in term. There is, alas, no way of knowing if Cranmer attended such classes, but their very existence must have stirred the university. Widespread interest would have been prompted in a visiting professor already convinced of the value of original languages as indispensable aids to understanding [**Extract 3**].

Cranmer certainly revised his grasp of such studies in due course, but before that he was claimed by an affair of the heart, marrying (in 1515) a maiden he met at the Dolphin Inn in Bridge Street (who was in all probability, the daughter of the proprietor). Joan conceived shortly afterwards, and was cared for by relatives at nearby St Ives as her confinement approached. Cranmer left Jesus to teach at Buckingham College. He went though a stressful period of fund-raising to provide for the little family, involving a journey from village-to-village that took toll of his time, before tragedy struck: his young wife dying in childbirth. Cruelly distorted, this sad little episode was later to be used in controversy by critics who showed Cranmer neither sympathy nor understanding [**Extract 4**]. Those who are aware of the hard facts of medieval life and death will realise that there is something of a commonplace in such a social setback, and they ought to make allowance for the subsequent predictable period of withdrawal by a scholar of all too human sensitivity.

When Jesus College renewed his fellowship, the positive assistance given to him unquestionably helped. He also found solace in further study and preparation for priesthood - he was ordained about 1520, though at this period his life is shrouded in mystery. That his scholarly reputation nevertheless grew in these years seems evident from an attempt to place Cranmer among a number of rising young Cambridge luminaries in the firmament of the newly founded Cardinal College, Oxford (1525). His refusal to accept this translation seems to have strengthened Cranmer's position with his Alma Mater, for, proceeding DD in 1526, he is listed as university examiner in divinity from this time. Erasmus's influential *Enchiridion* (first published at Antwerp in 1503) had already viewed the philosophy of Christ as a balanced blend of good and sacred letters [**Extract 5**]. Then too, the publication, and later revisions of *Novum instrumentum omne . . .* (1516), certainly brought many under the spell of 'the new divinity'. In a letter, to be found in P. S. Allen's collection (Vol. III, p. 177), Erasmus referred to *Cantabrigia mutata* and recorded that 'this School detests those chill subtleties which make more for disputation than for piety'. The *Enchiridion* was almost a trailer for *Novum instrumentum*, and in particular for *Ratio verae theologiae* (1518), where, in brief compass as a manifesto and tract for the times, Erasmus outlined the approach that transformed much theology and many a theologian in the Cambridge of Cranmer's day. The mists of speculative philosophy were receding and giving new light to a methodical discipline. This was primarily philological in approach, making a normative theology of Biblical exegesis. By careful concentration on scriptural texts, moreover, Erasmus and his 'Christian' humanist disciples pleaded that they were busily re-claiming all that was best in patristic learning.

From his own grasp of both scripture and the Fathers, it might seem logical to argue that Cranmer was just such a humanist. But historians should tread warily here for epithets like 'Erasmian' and 'Christian humanist', when used as generalised labels, are unwise and carry little meaning. Someone with a liberal education could display ancient learning in a way Dr Alistair Fox has described as 'a bravura flourish of classical *exempla*'. But humanists concerned themselves with form, style and substance, and not with the pastoral priorities of a positive programme of Church reform. Cranmer undoubtedly used textual criticism and exegesis to reclaim the plain sense of scripture and 'the old authors'; but the fact that he laid emphasis on the gospel as he understood it, rather than on any particular method of redis-covering the faith, is of singular significance. For while Erasmus attacked Church abuses and religious superstition in a language of urbane critique and caricature, Cranmer, once the opportunity came his way, would forge ahead and do what he could to remedy any situation he clearly deplored. In the ideal world of the humanist, classical learning glimpsed the glories of the past; but in the real world of the reformer, determined efforts were made to regain the faith laid down in scripture and ordered by the practice of the primitive Church.

In 1538, Cranmer might admittedly act the pedant with his prince [**Extract 6**], but that eccentric educational encounter precisely illus-trates the point under consideration. For by then, five years into his primacy, Cranmer was doing what he could in the face of opposition from bishops of 'the old religion' to implement new emphases in continental reform for an English formulary, the *Bishops' Book*. His exposition clearly prized the message far more than the method: an approach equally apparent in the ministry of the Swiss reformers Zwingli, Oecolampadius and Calvin, all of whom had no mean reputation as 'humanists'. Truly, as the Italian scholar Weiss stated in a contribution to the *New Cambridge Modern History*, the Reforma-tion proved 'both the culmination and the ruin of humanism'.

Extract 1

... as towching his education and bryngyng upp in his youthe. I have harde hymselfe reporte, that his father did sett hym to scole with a mervelous severe and cruell scolemaster. Whose tyranny towards youthe was suche, that, as he thoughte, the said scolemaster so appalled, dulled, and daunted the tender and fyne wittes of his scolers, that thei comonlie [more] hated and aborred good litterature than favored or inbraced the same, w[hose] memories were also therby so mutulated and wounded, that for his p[arte] he loste moche of that benefitt of memorey and audacitie in his youthe that by nature was given unto hym, whiche he could never recover, as he divers tymes reported . . . .

Item, after this his bringing upp at gramer-scole he was sent to the universitie of Cambridge, where for the most parte he remayned within Jesus colledge . . .

'Anecdotes and Character of Archbishop Cranmer', by Ralph Morice, his secretary; in *Narratives*, pp. 238-40.

Extract 2

Thomas Cranmer, the sonne of Thomas Cranmer of Aslocton esquier, and of Agnes Hatfield his wyefe, doughter of Laurence Hatfield of Wylloughby of lyke degre, was born (at the sayd Aslocton, within the county of Notingham) the second of July 1489, and learned his gramar of a rude parishe clerke in that barbarus tyme, unto his age of 14 yeares, and then he was sent by his seyd mother to Cambrege, where he was nosseled in the grossest kynd of sophistry, logike, philosophy morall and naturall (not in the text of the old philosophers, but chefely in the darke ridels and quidites of Duns and other subtile questionestes) to his age of xxij yeares. After that, he gave hymselfe to Faber, Erasmus, good Laten authors, iiij or v yeares togyther, unto the tyme that Luther began to wryte: and then he, considering what great contraversie was in matters of religion (not only in tryfles but in the cheefest articles of our salvation) bent himselfe to trye out the truthe herin: and, for as moche as he perceyved that he could not judge indifferently in so weyghty matters without the knowledge of the holy scriptures (before he were enfected with any mannes opinions or errours) he applyed his whole studye iiij yeares unto the seyd scryptures. After this he gave his mynde to good wryters both newe and old, not rashely running over them, for he was a slowe reader, but a diligent marker of whatsoever he redd, for he seldom redd without pen in hand, and whatsoever made eyther for the one parte or the other, of thinges being in contraversy, he wrote it out yf it were short, or at the least noted the author and the place, that he might fynd it and wryte it out by leysure; which was a great helpe to hym in debating of matters ever after. This kynde of studie he used till he were made doctor of divinitie, which was about the 34 of his age.

MS Harl. 417, fol. 90; in *Narratives, of the Days of the Reformation*, pp. 218-19.

Extract 3

Latin erudition, albeit ample, is stunted and incomplete without Greek. In Latin we have at best some brooks and murky pools, whilst they have crystal clear springs and rivers flowing with gold. I regard it as extreme insanity to touch with the little finger that focal point of theology dealing with the mysteries unless competence in Greek is also put to good use . . .

Erasmus to Antony of Bergen, March 1501; in *Erasmi Epistolae*, edited by P.S. Allen, Vol. 1, p. 352.

Extract 4

There was an infamy of hym, that he shoulde have byn an osteler, whiche the ignorante popishe preistes for very malice hadd published againste hym, saying that he had no maner of lernyng attalle more than ostelers arr wonte to have; and this rumour sprange of that, that when he hadd maried his firste wife, being reader than of Buckingham colledge, he did putt his wif to borde in an inne at Cambridge. And he resorting thether unto her in the inne, some ignorante preiste named hym to be the osteler, and his wif the tapster. This brute than began. But it moche more was quickened when he was archebisshopp than before. Insomoche that a preiste farr northe, about Scarbarowe, syttyng emonges his neighbours at the alehouse and talking of the archeb-isshopp Cranmer, divers men there moche commending hym, 'What! (saicd the preiste) make ye somoche of hym? he was but an osteler, and hath asmoche lernyng as thc gooslynges of the grene that goo yender'.

Narratives, p. 269

Extract 5

. . . It has taken a long time and many a battle to come to these opinions. It is perhaps a presumptuous thing to do. Nevertheless, we rely on God's assistance and carefully devote our attention to it. After Origen, Ambrose, Augustine, and so many more modern interpret-ers we certainly shall not be alone in the task, and following them, we do not think that our effort will be entirely fruitless.

There are certain detractors, who think that true religion has nothing to do with good literature [*bonae literae*]. May I state that I have been studying the Classics [ancient literature] since my youth; and not without much burning of midnight oil have gained a working knowledge of both Greek and Latin. This I did not undertake merely for empty fame or childish pleasures of the mind. Rather was my sole purpose that, knowing these writings, I could the better adorn the Lord's Temple with literary treasures. Too many in recent times, through ignorance and boorishness, have been doing the exact opposite. Through this type of study a man's generous natural qualities can be enflamed with a love of Holy Scripture.

Erasmus, *Enchiridion Militis Christiani* (1503), concluding paragraph.

Extract 6

v. 'By his grace and mercy.' This obscureth the sentence, and is superfluous: for it is sufficiently expressed by the former words, that is to say, 'by his mere goodness only.'

vi. 'By his ordinance.' This also obscureth the sense, and is superfluous.

vii. 'Ordained.' The preter tense may not conveniently be joined with the present tense. . . .

xvii. 'I doing my duty.' We may not say that we do our duty. Nevertheless he hath not the right faith in his heart, that hath not a good heart and will to do his duty; . . . But no man doth do all his duty, for then he needeth not to have any faith for the remission of his sins. Therefore this particle following 'that all my sins be washed away.'

xxxix. 'To the intent that they may thereby attain certain comfort and consolation of their consciences.' Although these words make the sentences not very perfect in English, yet they may stand: but I like it better as it is in the print. . . .

xliii. 'To consecrate sacraments.' Consecration is called only of the sacrament of the altar: therefore it is more plain to say thus: 'to consecrate the body of Christ, and to minister the sacraments.' . . .

l. 'Or honour them as God or Gods.' We may not thus add to the words of scripture, but set them out first plainly and surely, even as they be, and after expound and declare them. . . .

lv. 'Priests and bishops.' If these words be added, then this sentence joineth not well with the sentence following. And if any man be offended with this word 'preach', then if it be put out, and this word 'teach' put in the stead thereof after this sort, 'and we must also teach', then do both the sentences run in a good composition together, so that no man can be offended.

The Renaissance World of Learning

Selections from 'Corrections of the *Institution of a Christian Man*, by Henry VIII, with Archbishop Cranmer's Annotations'; in *Cranmer II*, pp. 83 ff. The extracts illustrate not merely Cranmer's correction of Henry's prose (and so the archbishop's superb sense of style), but also his readiness to put the prince right in matters of theology.

2
Court and Embassy

There is a medieval 'wandering scholar' dimension to Cranmer's career between 1529 and 1533.

First, early in 1529, an outbreak of the plague in Cambridge coincided with a plea from Waltham for a tutor to the Cressy boys, whose mother was related to the Nottinghamshire Cranmers. Although the sickness on the Cam had subsided by the high summer and Cranmer had returned to Cambridge, he went back to Waltham in July to enjoy further hospitality from his friends. At that time the king happened to visit the district to enjoy the pleasures of the chase. By a curious chance, two high-ranking members of the royal retinue, both of them to play significant roles [Secretary Gardiner and Almoner Fox], found accommodation with the Cressys. There must have been something of a 'Let Dons delight' supper party at which contact between the three Cambridge men was renewed. Their conversation doubtless turned on reminiscence and university affairs as well as on that burning issue of the hour, the king's 'privy matter'. For an established theologian (Dr Thomas Cranmer was just 40 years of age), here was a rare opportunity to forward the claims of his academic discipline at a moment when many in high places had begun to despair of the delaying tactics of canon lawyers in the *cause célèbre*. If his insistence that university opinion could resolve the 'divorce' was not new, it was nonetheless welcomed by both Gardiner and Fox, who probably suggested he set out his case with due care. For it was not long before Henry sought a Cambridge view. Arguably it was his recognition of Cranmer's role in persuading most of his colleagues to support the Crown (rather than the martyrologist John Foxe's supposed 'next day' summons owing to the inspiration of a fellow of Jesus College at dinner) that first brought Cranmer into the royal presence at Greenwich in October that year.

Secondly, it was, of course, the impression Cranmer made at

Court, and in particular the academic support he gave the royal cause, that prompted Henry to send him to Italy with the Earl of Wiltshire's embassy in 1530. Immediately after his first meeting with the king, it would seem that Cranmer went to live at Durham House, the London home of the Boleyns in the Strand, and there, from scripture and the 'old authors', he compiled his case in support of 'the divorce'. Ralph Morice glossed the occasion - as he could not have had first-hand knowledge - in quaint and general terms:

And after some special communication with the said Dr Cranmer, the King retained him to write his mind in that his cause of divorcement, and committed him unto the Earl of Wiltshire, Queen Anne's father, to be entertained of him at Durham Place, where the Earl did lie, until he had penned his mind and opinion concerning the said cause (*Narratives*, p. 242).

A Renaissance prince, Henry had developed a taste for 'the new learning' and, encouraged by what he had read of Cranmer's arguments, may well have sent him with the earl in case an opportunity presented itself to introduce the Emperor to the 'wonderfully virtuous and wise man' (*ung merbvilleux et serieulx sage homme*) he had enlisted. Whatever the truth of the matter, Cranmer and Charles V did not meet. The imperial coronation took place at Bologna on 24 February, and the English delegation only arrived there on 14 March. Nor is it even certain that Cranmer went to Bologna, for he reached Rome in April to serve the traditional spell as grand penitentiary for England during an approved period of residence at the papal court. His purpose was defence of the Tudor policy regarding the King's marriage, but, frustrated by imperial objections, the pope only sanctioned inquiry by canon lawyers and theologians on 4 August. The dilemma that disturbed Henry and Catherine was held by Clement VII to be a proper subject for investigation, but he wanted argument and conscience to determine the outcome, not the use of 'retainers' (a clear indication that the Curia was well-informed of the shameless way in which bribes were influencing opinion at Ferrara, Bologna, Padua and elsewhere). Although clearly frustrated in his principal objective, when Cranmer left Rome towards the end of September he had nevertheless gained the kind of insights that were to prove invaluable.

Thirdly, after a year's experience and much further study, Dr Cranmer was despatched to Regensburg as ambassador (*consiliarius regius*) to the Court of Charles V. Albeit charged with championing

Henry's cause before the emperor, he was expected to concern himself even more with the Protestant princes. The Turk presented a real threat to Vienna, and at such a time it was thought that an English alliance with the Protestants might well commend itself by strengthening both sides against the emperor. But everything went wrong: Charles was afflicted with gout; the Turk seemed likely to triumph. Fearful of the consequences if the Empire yielded to the infidel, the princes rallied so convincingly at this time of crisis that Cranmer could see he was wasting his time. Nevertheless, with Nürnberg only fifty miles from Regensburg, contact was established with the Lutheran princes there. This may have brought no return for Henry's cause, for Luther was himself opposed to the idea of the divorce and had written to Robert Barnes on the subject at some length in September 1531 [**Extract 1**]; but in his private capacity the king's ambassador had gained first-hand experience of the Protestant religion, its faith and practice.

When Cranmer consulted Andreas Osiander (Hosmer) of Nürnberg, that pastor (although he did not follow Luther's line, arguing instead that Julius II's dispensation of 1503, which allowed Henry and Catherine to marry, was illegal), preferred to keep his views to himself and avoid any open show of disloyalty to the emperor. On another matter Cranmer himself was far from secretive, for it was at this time that he married Margaret, niece of Frau Osiander. The move was a bold one in so far as it openly flouted canon law: Cranmer's priesthood denied him the right to marry. That he did marry regardless indicates both his conviction that scripture took precedence over church law and, indeed, that Lutheran theology had already made an impact on him.

If his time at the embassy had given him a wife and domestic happiness, contact with leading Lutherans such as John Frederick, the new elector of Ernestine Saxony, and his chaplain-secretary, Spalatin, brought lasting insight into German ways and values. Cranmer's own interest in hunting, perhaps extended during his time as ambassador, certainly prompted the advice he gave two years later in a letter to Cromwell, namely that, despite his name, Lewis the Pacific, the Elector Palatine, would greatly prefer a gift of hunting dogs to jewels [**Extract 2**]. Another experience remote from academic life came Dr Cranmer's way that same autumn (1532). Through treaty obligations, Charles was entitled to support from the English king at a time of emergency, and because of this Cranmer followed the imperial progress from Regensburg to Vienna, passing on despatches to the French-Burgundian Nicolas Perrenot, seigneur de Granvelle, as they came to hand from England. Before embarking on his voyage down the Danube, Cranmer let Henry VIII know that his latest briefing in the matter of 'the divorce' had reached Regensburg with Paget and had been relayed to the emperor in writing at Granvelle's request. He reported that there would perhaps be an answer at Linz, which he expected to reach before Charles V. The despatch provided a general bulletin of European events for English consumption, and made particular reference to the reformation of faith, and to the taxes the emperor planned to levy [**Extract 3**].

Cranmer sent his report from Regensburg on 4 September, and much had happened by 20 October when he wrote again from Villach on the Austro-Italian border. Briefly, Süleyman's attempt to revenge his 1529 setback at Vienna had failed, largely because his forces were again delayed by the siege of Güns-Köszeg. With huge distances to cover, even crack regiments had to be restricted to seasonal operations or suffer disaster from bad weather and weakened lines of communication. Nevertheless such a challenge had caused the Hapsburgs real concern, and following Charles V's urgent call to arms an immense and well-equipped force had been mobilised near Vienna. At the end of a summer of sorties rather than any concentrated campaign, Süleyman deemed September to be a time for tactical withdrawal and he fell back on Carinthia and Croatia. When Charles chose in turn to conclude hostilities, many unpaid troops preferred mutiny to demobilisation. In the subsequent anarchy Cranmer turned war correspondent. Henry VIII thus learnt how Spanish and Italian troops wrought far worse devastation on the Austrian countryside than had the Turk, provoking the peasantry (the 'boors') into a guerrilla-style response [**Extract 4**]. His letter also explained to the English king that Charles, *en route* for Spain, intended to confer with the pope in Italy: 'I do think that he will not forget to make mention ... of your grace's great cause ...' Cranmer the ambassador was also at work and anxious to 'be instructed of your pleasure what I shall do.' (*Cranmer II*, pp. 232-3) In fact, of course, when those instructions reached Cranmer they gave him the surprise of his life. For Archdeacon Nicholas Hawkins brought word to Mantua that Thomas Cranmer had been named to succeed the octogenarian Warham (who had died on 23 August) as archbishop of Canterbury.

Extract 1

My Anthony: here you finally have also my opinion on the case of the King of England, since you insist on it with such great perseverance.

To begin with . . . I approve of the decision of the faculty of Louvain . . . and the King may abide by it with a sufficiently safe conscience; in fact he has to abide by it if he wants to be on the safe side. Under no circumstances will he be free to divorce the Queen to whom he is married, the wife of his deceased brother, and thus make the mother as well as the daughter into incestuous women. Even if the King might have sinned by marrying the wife of his deceased brother, and even if the dispensation granted by the Roman pope might not have been valid (I do not debate this now), nevertheless it would be a heavier and more dreadful sin to divorce the woman he had married; and this especially for the reason that then the King, as well as the Queen and the Young Queen [the princess Mary], could be forever charged with, and considered as, being incestuous people. According to my opinion, therefore, those who urge the King to the divorce for this reason alone torture his conscience in vain. If he has sinned by marrying, then this sin is past, and like all other sins of the past is amended through repentance; but the marriage should not be torn apart for this reason, and such a heavy future sin ought not to be permitted. For how many marriages are there in the world which have been made through sinning? And yet they ought not and may not be put asunder. So much for this one reason.

Regarding the other reason - whether you are fabricating it, or whether it is true - that the King is searching for a son, an heir to the kingdom, but that the Queen gives birth only to girls, etc. . . . Who doesn't see that this is an even less valid argument? Who will assure the King either that this present Queen will not give birth to a boy (if age does not hinder it), or that the other Queen, the one whom he is to marry, will give birth to boys? Nevertheless, even if it would be certain that the other Queen would give birth to boys, it still will not be permissable to divorce the former Queen, especially not as an incestuous women, and thus equally to put the mark of incest forever on the offspring, that is, to punish them without any cause with this extremely heavy punishment. Before I would approve of such a divorce I would rather permit the King to marry still another woman and to have, according to the examples of the patriarchs and kings, two women or queens at the same time.

Martin Luther to Robert Barnes [*Antonius Anglus*], from Wittenberg, 3 September 1531; in *LW*, Vol. 50, pp. 31-3.

Extract 2

Right worshipful Mr Crumwell, in my right hearty wise I commend me to you. And where the county Palantyne amonges all other pleasures doth much esteem the pastime of hunting with great greyhounds, and especially with great mastiffs, which in those parties be had in great price and value: these therefore be to pray to you to advertise the king's highness to send unto the said county a couple or two of great greyhounds, and as many of great mastiffs: the same shall be as well accepted to him as though it had pleased his grace to have sent him a precious jewel or reward; which thing shall be no great charge to his grace, and yet nevertheless shall be highly esteemed with the receiver of the same. And therefore I pray you to have this thing in your special remembrance, when ye shall have convenient time.

Cranmer to Cromwell, from Otford, 10 June 1534; in *Cranmer II*, p. 296.

Extract 3

... when the said Monsieur Grandeveile inquired of me, if I had any answer of the aid and subsidy which the emperor desired of your grace, I reported unto him fully your grace's answer, according unto mine instructions sent unto me by your grace's servant, William Paget. Which answer he desired me to deliver him in writing, that he might refer the same truly unto the emperor; and so I did. Nevertheless the emperor now at his departing, hath had such importune business, that Monsieur Grandeveile assigned me to repair unto the emperor again at Lyntz; for there, he said, I shall have an answer again in writing. The French ambassador and I with all diligence do make preparation to furnish ourselves of wagons, horses, ships, tents, and other things necessary to our voyage; but it will be at the least eight or ten days before we can be ready to depart hence. Yet we trust to be at Lyntz before the emperor; for he will tarry by the way at Passaw ten or twelve days.

As for the Turk, he resideth still in Hungary in the same place environed upon all parts, whereof I wrote unto your highness in my last letters. And the emperor departed from Abagh toward Vienna the second day of this month by land, not coming by this town; but the same day king Ferdinando departed from this town by water, and at Passaw, fourteen miles hence, they shall meet, and so pass forth unto Lyntz, which is the midway from hence unto Vienna. And there the emperor will tarry to counsel what he will do: and there all the ambassadors shall know his pleasure, as Monsieur Grandeveile shewed me.

I have sent herewith unto your grace the copy of the emperor's proclamation concerning a general council, and a reformation to be had in Germany for the controversies of the faith. Also I have sent the tax of all the states of the empire, how many soldiers every man is limited unto for the aid against the Turk. Wherein your grace may perceive, that the greatest prince in Germany (only the duke of Burgundy and Austry except) is not appointed above 120 horsemen and 554 footmen. Thus our Lord evermore have your highness in his preservation and governance.

Cranmer to Henry VIII, from Regensburg, 4 September 1532; in *Cranmer II*, p. 232.

Extract 4

As touching the emperor's army of Italians and Spaniards that came out of Italy in their coming to Vienna . . . they have done great damage unto all the countries that they have passed by, as I wrote unto your highness in my last letters, dated the second day of this month; but now, in returning again into Italy by another way through Austria, Stiria, and Carinthia, the Italians have done much more harm. For eight thousand of them . . . for indignation that the emperor would not prosecute the Turk, and for lack of payment of their wages, departed from the emperor and from their captains, and chose captain among themselves, and went before the emperor, spoiling and robbing all the countries . . . more than two hundredth English miles in length, as well churches as other houses, not leaving monstral nor the sacrament. And the men of arms that come with the emperor, and other that follow the court, do con[sume] all that the other left, in such sort, that I, following two days after the emperor from Vienna, found in no town that was unwalled man, woman, nor child, meat, drink, nor bedding; but, thanked be God! I found straw, hay, and corn, for my horses to eat, and for myself and my servant to lie in, but the people were all fled into [the] mountains for fear.

The said Italians not only robbed the towns, but also ravished the [wo]men, and beat the men, and slew many. . . . Of this sacking and brenning is like to ensue great penury and default of all victuals, and specially of corn; forasmuch as the corn here is brent up, whereupon the people should live this year, and sow their land against the next year. Thus is the country miserably oppressed of all parties, but much more by them that came to defend this country, than it was by the Turks. . . .

And now the husbandmen of this country be in such a tumultuation for the loss of their goods and the brenning of their houses, that they muster together upon the mountains, and with guns and stones do slay many of the emperor's people. And in divers places they come down from the mountains in the night, and do slay all the small companies that they may find sleeping. And many times they come down in the day in good companies, and rob carriages that do follow the court, and slay as many as will withstand them: so much that they have slain many gentlemen of the court; . . . But the boors put no difference between one man and another, for all that go with the emperor be to them Italians and Spaniards. . . .

Cranmer to Henry VIII, from Villach, 20 October 1532; in *Cranmer II*, pp. 233-4.

3
Henry's Archbishop

Although history finds nothing unusual in the preferment to prelacy of a little-known priest, the elevation of a mere archdeacon to the historic eminence of Canterbury's primatial see in 1533 was remarkable for its very rapidity. That Cranmer would in time have gained due reward for counsel at Court and service abroad is not in question; but to enter the bright light of royal favour when he had scarcely emerged from the mists of donnish obscurity was noteworthy by any reckoning. Nor had high politics at a particularly complex period of his reign prompted the almost desperate Henry to seek relief from a game of Russian roulette. Though it was most certainly urged on him by the Boleyn faction, Henry's nomination of Cranmer was nevertheless contrived by and convincing to the monarch himself.

Determined to do his duty by both realm and dynasty and provide a legitimate male heir, Henry had been sadly frustrated when, after no fewer than five unsuccessful pregnancies, Catherine gave birth to the Princess Mary on 18 February 1516. Genuinely concerned for religion as he was - even to the extent of writing against the Luther he felt, with all the conviction of a lay theologian, to be *advocatus diaboli* - it seemed to Henry that, however regular his devotion at Mass, his marriage was somehow blighted. Accordingly, he who once parried the qualified congratulation of an ambassador with the pertinent comment, 'We are both young; if it was a daughter this time, by the grace of God the sons will follow', was no longer capable of such a philosophical attitude. Instead he became convinced that by taking his brother's wife, he had contravened divine law. In short, the more Catherine miscarried, the more Henry's concern about the validity of his position grew. That doubt hardened into the ultimate conviction that, because of illicit union with the widow of his elder brother, Arthur, the king stood condemned for that breach of holy living set out in the code of Leviticus (Leviticus 20: 21): 'If a man take his brother's wife, it is an unclean thing ... they shall be childless.' The text of that law had become true for Henry, and, despite the papal guarantee already provided to the House of Tudor by Julius II's 1503 dispensation of affinity restriction, the king was convinced that he had no prince to succeed him because in God's sight he was living in sin.

The quest for 'divorce' that began in 1527 is only one aspect of royal policy in a period that because of its complexity has unique fascination. Though quaintly termed the king's 'privy matter', the issue soon involved Court and country, continent and Curia. Once ecclesiastical authority determined to oppose the royal petition, the issue widened from anxiety about the succession to embrace concepts of sovereignty and empire. It was a time when the opportunism of the king both fostered and devoured factions at Court, a crucial period when only solution of so pressing a problem could provide some sort of settled policy. Certainly, if the pope would not let Henry have his way, that defiant Tudor threatened to take the law into his own hands. It soon became clear that, in the vexed matter of Henry's marriage to Catherine, Clement VII was not prepared to jeopardise his papacy by a decision that would humiliate a close relative of the emperor himself: Catherine was his aunt.

At Blackfriars, Wolsey's legatine court failed to secure a decision for the king, Queen Catherine having prolonged Henry's frustration by making an appeal to Rome. As Shakespeare expressed it later:

I do refuse you for my judge, and here,
  Before you all, appeal unto the pope,
To bring my whole cause 'fore his holiness,
And to be judg'd by him.

But Henry refused her appeal and, with Anne Boleyn already in the wings, was passionate in his search for a policy that could repudiate the opposition ranged against him. Not that there was any shortage of available options. As long ago as 1515, his own royal judgement had assured Henry that 'kings of England in time past have never had any superior but God alone'. Then there was William Tyndale who, although he followed Luther in his opposition to the actual 'divorce' issue, nevertheless afforded the royal cause unqualified scriptural support in a fundamental argument in his *Obedience of a Christian Man*, a convincing tract of 1528 that placed 'the king ... in this world, without law', for the king 'may at his lust do right or wrong, and shall give accounts but to God only'. Another significant source of ideology at this time was the work of an elderly bencher of the Middle Temple, Christopher St German. A potent theorist, his views across the whole spectrum of life in Church and State had the compelling clarity that can shake the very foundations of society. In *Doctor and Student*, St German made much of a scriptural authority this time enhanced because of early Church approval. For him it was the key authority that underwrote the power of princes. A shrewd observer of clerical pretensions, moreover, St German, from the standpoint of common, rather than canon, law, urged secular not spiritual supremacy and declared the king in parliament to be: 'the high sovereign over the people which hath not only charge on the bodies but also on the souls of his subjects'. Then there was Edward Fox, royal almoner and later bishop of Hereford (1535), who had become a forceful 'firebrand on the divorce issue', in the opinion of the imperial ambassador, Chapuys. Sometime Provost of King's College, Cambridge, Fox was a theologian by training and a staunch supporter of Anne Boleyn. Accordingly, much was afoot before the royal cause gained a significant accession of strength with the administrative genius and organising ability of Thomas Cromwell. In the words of Professor Eric Ives in *Anne Boleyn* (pp. 186-7), 'Tyndale's unitary sovereign state, Fox's supreme headship, St German's King-in-parliament - here already is the philosophy, the proclamation and the mechanism of the Henrician Reformation'.

Fox had involved Cranmer in a considerable compilation that, drawn from scriptural and patristic texts, consiliar decrees, legal judgements and early chronicles, unquestionably supported Henry's cause. This was *Collectanea satis copiosa* (c. 1530), a manuscript that, to judge from excited marginal queries, clearly gained royal approval, Henry's '*Ubi hic*' [whence this?] showing how zealous he, with his Renaissance mind, was to make use of old material the scholars had brought to hand. By his shrewd analysis of the *Collectanea*, Dr Graham Nicholson has shed a bright shaft of light on the way Tudor scholars provided their king and his closest policy-makers with background data crucial to the attainment of royal sovereignty in England. From an amazing assortment of source materials, several different hands wrote out and compiled more than a hundred folio pages of proof texts chosen to confound, and calculated to damage, established doctrines of papal supremacy. Notions circulated at Court, that in themselves were slender enough as evidence, once accumulated, made the required impact. There was, for example, Aelred's record that King Edgar had seen fit to reprove clerical immorality. Pope Eleutherius counselled King Lucius (a soundly converted but altogether mythical monarch) to rule by divine law rather than by Rome or Caesar. And William of Malmesbury was quoted to confirm the fact that, in Aethelstan's day, the pope taught the faith by royal authority. In the early 1530s, therefore, to quote Dr Nicholson, 'the sudden talk, first of the privileges of the realm and then of empire, from Norfolk, Wiltshire, Suffolk and the king himself was . . . a slightly less than coherent version of Fox's carefully documented theories of church and state'. And again: 'There existed as early as 1530 the germ, at least, of a theory of empire, which is seen fully grown in the Act of Appeals in 1533.'

Dr Nicholson's article 'The Act of Appeals and the English reformation' in *Law and Government under the Tudors* (CUP 1988) mentions Merlin's edition *Quatuor conciliorum generalium*, as 'a major source for the *Collectanea*' (p. 25). Dr Nicholson also refers to the section of references that drew on decrees of early provincial councils and letters of Pope Leo that 'show kings summoning and dominating synods and giving confirmation to the edicts and laws enacted' as a 'late addition to the *Collectanea*' (p. 28). Circumstantial evidence indicates that this late addition was the work of Fox, whose 'public career was from the beginning linked with the divorce'. Later, it was certainly Fox who drew on such heavy textual material when he wrote his *Opus eximium de vera differentia* (1534) in defence of the royal ecclesiastical supremacy. But what is not so widely known is Thomas Cranmer's contribution.

When Fox and Gardiner first discussed the king's 'privy matter' with Cranmer at Waltham, circumstantial evidence suggests they concerned themselves with securing university opinion, and subsequent events indicate that Cranmer busied himself in that work. But academic judgements would not have provided any profound in-put to the royal think-tank, at least not at a level of ideology potent enough to forward revolutionary change in Church - State relations of the kind Henry and his closest counsellors were beginning to contemplate. However sympathetic he was towards the 'divorce', the donnish Cranmer would have been viewed as something of a soft touch at Court; and with worldly-wise prelates like John Stokesley, Edward Lee, Stephen Gardiner and Edward Fox himself as rivals, he would not have seemed a serious candidate for so crucial an appointment when Warham died. That he was selected after a five-month delay suggests that there was some convincing evidence of his commitment to the cause at an altogether deeper level than either his influence on university opinion or his efficiency in ambassadorial service.

Although historians are unlikely ever to know the complete truth of the matter, a Sotheby's auction has opened up new lines of inquiry. In 1985 a copy of Merlin's *Quatuor conciliorum generalium* was bought by a Californian collector. This was no ordinary tome; the volume belonged to Cranmer and contains almost two hundred marginal notes and underlinings in his hand. Of great significance too is the fact that this is the first edition of Merlin's work, published at Paris in 1524, whereas that used by Edward Fox was the Cologne printing of 1530. It seems that Cranmer almost certainly knew of Merlin in his Cambridge days, possibly even before he proceeded to the doctorate (1526) and took a turn at examining. Precise dating of Cranmer's possession and initial use of Merlin is difficult to ascertain, but as little of the marginal material is related to the 'divorce' issue, an early date is possible. Moreover, his notes on Pope Innocent and the Council of Carthage - written alongside *De libero arbitrio contra Pelagium et Celestinum* - could perhaps reflect the great debate between Luther and Erasmus on the freedom or bondage of the human will in 1525, especially from one so knowledgeable about continental *causes célèbres* as Dr Cranmer. Be that as it may, Cranmer's fascination with Merlin would have related to that editor's inclusion in his collection of a number of conciliar canons and early papal letters which Renaissance enthusiasm mistakenly attributed to Isidore of Seville. It seems that at this time of revival of interest in the early Fathers, Cranmer was excited by this new cache of documents that added to his understanding of the faith and practice of the early Church. Merlin's preface attempted to rally Christian leaders to the cause. Let them learn from primitive precept and practice and be wary of heresy. Now when he was himself busily engaged in the task of sifting scripture through the Fathers, Cranmer undoubtedly enthused over 'blessed Isidorus' and the new scope Merlin's anthology gave him.

That he used the compilation in a different way from Fox is also clear from many *marginalia* contained in his copy. At this time, for example, Cranmer (ordained as a priest in c.1520), was concerned to know whether the early Church had permitted its priests to marry, and a number of references and textual underlining relate to the subject of clergy wives (*De clericu*[m] *uxorib*[us]). Secondly, although he shows respect for Peter the apostle - there is a reference to *Ius sancti Petri* - Cranmer is already dubious about the popes being regarded as the successors to Peter. A note on a letter of Pope Clement, when translated from the abbreviated medieval Latin, runs 'If these words apply to the successors of Clement, I ask whether the Pope is a heretic?' And when he comes across a letter of Clement on clerical responsibilities - the text uses an analogy to argue that the apostle likened the truth of the word to the rays of the sun in its enlightenment of men's minds - Cranmer's marginal note inquires, 'Where are these words of Peter written?' Thirdly, although much careful textual work has yet to be resolved, it would seem that Cranmer's marginal notes indicate a searching interest in early examples of the determination of disputes by provincial synods, from which there was no appeal. For example, the Council of Nicaea states that 'matters ought to be concluded in the province where they arose'; and his marginal notes include cross-references to the Councils of Antioch and Constantinople and to the apostolic canons. Later too, with reference to a decretal of Julius, Cranmer records an instance of papal distortion of scripture which he deplores, and of Nicene deliberations that 'did not relate to the Council . . . unless he [the pope] adds it on his own'. Elsewhere, Cranmer carefully dates the councils, and for ease of reference repeats the names of significant Latin and Greek Fathers (Ambrose, Athanasius, Augustine ['*Beatus Augustinus*'], Gregory of Nazianzus, Gregory of Nyssa, Chrysostom, Hilary, Dionysius, Cyril) in the margins. Clearly his interest is markedly different from that which was shown by Edward Fox later, though the reader gains from a whole range of scholarly comment (and from references like '*Lex papa*') an overall impression of his anti-papal attitude.

Can such circumstantial evidence help the historian to get more of the measure of Cranmer in these early days? An affirmative answer is certainly possible, but it must be very carefully qualified, for much close textual work lies ahead. Nevertheless some new facts clearly emerge. In the first place, Cranmer's possession and annotation of the 1524 edition could mean he worked on the Merlin volume before Fox. Secondly, however, cautious scrutiny reveals that Cranmer put the material to a specifically theological use, namely to serve the purpose discernible in the manuscript collections on the early councils (now held by the Marquess of Salisbury at Hatfield House), of which this was clearly a prime source. It was surely this material the archbishop had in mind when, after he had been in office for some time, and was writing against the Devon rebels, he referred to 'sundry old canons, decrees and councils' (*Cranmer II*, p. 169). The phrase is one that neatly complements Cromwell's celebrated 'divers sundry old authentic histories and chronicles', for together they symbolise the two sides of the medal that was the royal ecclesiastical supremacy. A final point is noteworthy, namely that Cranmer evidently held unorthodox views on various issues at an earlier date than historians have usually recognised; and that fact - although it might have caused the traditional Catholic conscience of Henry VIII some concern - must surely have commended Cranmer to the Boleyns, whose success in explaining any taint of 'heresy' in specifically anti-papal terms finally convinced the king. In short, Henry came to realise that he had in Thomas Cranmer precisely the man he desperately needed not merely to solve his pressing 'privy matter', but above all to serve him with unquestioning loyalty and obedience as 'godly prince' and supreme head of a sovereign Church in his own kingdom. Although this time in reverse, the medieval principle of suitability had been well and truly applied.

When it came to Cranmer's consecration, Henry's officials left nothing to chance. If the Curia failed to grant the customary bulls, and both to confirm the new primate and confer the pallium that symbolised his plenitude of power, annates (a tax the clergy were obliged to pay to Rome on appointment to office, already conditionally withheld by Act of Parliament in March 1532), would be permanently withdrawn. When that statute also made it clear that attempts to delay or failure to grant bulls would result in consecration regardless, Rome realised the extent of such a threat and, although there was some haggling over the expenses incurred, the Curia did everything to curry favour with an English king who meant business. For his part, Henry indulged Cranmer at an expensive time and lent him about £1,000, quite apart from the moneys (about which Chapuys wrote to inform the emperor) forwarded to Rome to secure the bulls. Just over a month later, on 30 March 1533, Cranmer was consecrated bishop in the Chapter House of Westminster Abbey. Although March was a canonical season for ordinations, and the consecration of a bishop could only take place on a Sunday, no major festival or saint's day was selected for the occasion, the authorities concerning themselves with speed rather than any special sanctity. John Voysey of Exeter and Henry Standish of St Asaph presented the bishop-elect to John Longland of Lincoln as consecrator, the two assistants holding the gospels over Cranmer's neck before his head and hands were consecrated with the chrism and holy oil. Though he was then presented with the insignia of staff, ring and mitre, and took the customary oath to the pope, Cranmer was prepared in conscience by the terms of a previous protestation he had made in the chapter house of the abbey church [**Extract 1**]. Furthermore, he stated in forthright terms that, 'before Almighty God and the holy Evangelists', his oath of obedience to the pope was subject to precisely that qualification. A furore has inevitably raged over the matter almost since the day Cranmer took his oaths. Yet in a general historical context there is nothing untoward here; the new primate was taking these vows precisely because he was required to do so. If Henry was to make full use of his new position as *summus pontifex Angliae*, consecration that fully accorded with the traditions of Rome and the canon law had to obtain. There would have been little point in the Crown incurring such time, trouble and expense in procuring Cranmer's bulls if at the last Henry merely secured a bishop uncanonical - whose judgements would go unrecognised. For his part, Cranmer, perhaps beginning to grasp the ways of the world, must have been counselled by the king's closest advisers that it was in his best interests to make a solemn pledge of loyalty to the pope, and indeed that in the circumstances Henry required that of him. The essential background to the whole episode was the 1532 submission of the clergy and the king's calculated words to Mr Speaker on 11 May before a combination of pressures brought Convocation to heel four days later:

> Well beloved subjects, we thought that the clergy of our realm had been our subjects wholly, but now we have well perceived that they be but half our subjects, yea, and scarce our subjects: for all the prelates at their consecration make an oath to the pope, clean contrary to the oath that they make to us, so that they seem to be his subjects and not ours . . .
>
> Edward Hall, *Chronicle of Henry VIII*, Vol. II, p. 210.

Although Cranmer's oath has been interpreted as a principled protest it was undoubtedly prudent in the circumstances. Historians who remain convinced that the new primate committed perjury on the very day he assumed high spiritual office might more profitably ponder the wording of the ancient oath archbishops customarily took to the Crown for Canterbury's temporalities, an oath Cranmer himself took on 19 April [**Extract 2**].

If Cranmer had convinced himself that he was bound to accept papal jurisdiction only when that accorded with scriptural authority, twelve days after his consecration those same principles were exercised in the matter of the 'divorce'. For on Good Friday, no less, he wrote a memorable letter humbly begging leave 'to proceed to the examination, final determination, and judgement in the said great cause, touching Your Highness'[Extract 3]. Henry had secretly married Anne Boleyn some time towards the end of January, her pregnancy finally forcing the king to take the relationship seriously in his quest for a legitimate heir. Years later, at his Oxford trial, Cranmer made it clear that 'no man can serve two masters at once'; and when he convened his court at Dunstable Priory he soon showed where his loyalty lay. Thomas Cromwell's celebrated Act in Restraint of Appeals had passed into law in April 1533 so that Catherine's cause was effectively lost before it began. Cranmer nevertheless went dutifully through his allotted task, being considerably relieved when the queen, nearby at Ampthill, refused to answer his summons. For her contempt Catherine was pronounced *vere et manifeste contumacem*, and once she had been barred from appearing, it was with evident ease of mind that the king's 'most humble beadman and chaplain' wrote on 12 May to inform Henry that he would now 'make more acceleration and expedition in my process than I thought I should' (*Cranmer II*, p. 241). On 17 and 23 May two further letters kept the king posted, revealing his primate's evident delight that 'to the pleasure of Almighty God, and the mere truth of the matter' Henry's dilemma had at last been resolved. That rejoicing was in order, too, related to 'the time of the coronation' now 'so instant and so near at hand' (*Cranmer II*, pp. 242, 244).

The coronation, the very seal and symbol of a true marriage that made a lawful queen of the Marchioness of Pembroke, took place in Westminster Abbey on the feast of Pentecost (1 June). Much moved by the pomp, circumstance and splendour of the first royal occasion over which he presided, to 'set the crown on her head', Cranmer wrote an account of the memorable event to Nicholas Hawkins, his successor as ambassador at the court of Charles V. It is an important letter, not least because its reference to Henry's marriage 'about St Paul's day last' scotched dangerous rumours that, at Dunstable, Cranmer had determined at law the validity of a marriage he had himself conducted [Extract 4].

In Rome barely a month later, Clement VII threatened excommunication; and although the pope was temporarily generous with the English king in the matter of that ultimate ecclesiastical sanction,

Henry's strong reaction amounted to severance of diplomatic relations. The king recalled Benet, Carne and Bonner, and in November he appealed to a general council of the Church. That same year, too Parliament made absolute the hitherto conditional Restraint of Annates; and in 1534 a list of significant statutes - that is, measures determining the succession (with application in terms of treason law), the submission of the clergy, dispensations and supremacy (again with backing in new treason legislation) - carried through, with all the compelling logic Cromwell could command, proclaimed a complete break with Rome. No longer was it heresy to criticise papal authority, and in 1536 by the Act Extinguishing [his] Authority, the supreme pontiff was reduced to the ranks as merely bishop of Rome.

The strategy and significance of such epoch-making change has long been at the heart of Sir Geoffrey Elton's massive contribution to Tudor studies. In his turn, Professor Scarisbrick has shed further light on the political and constitutional complexity of an altogether fascinating period of English history, light now further intensified by important re-assessments from Professor Eric Ives, Dr Alistair Fox, Dr John Guy, and, most recently, Dr Henry Chadwick.

Such authorities excel in their analysis of the ambiguity of Henry's supremacy over the English Church, and their often complex legal and constitutional arguments are the very stuff of scholarship. Cranmer's concern, by contrast, stemmed from his grasp of scripture, an understanding he carefully measured against the judgements of the early Church, its councils and Fathers. Accordingly, when Henry VIII blustered and bullied in his Tudor way to impose full power over the Church as a kind of royal peculiar, Cromwell did his best to make the English Church subject to the king in Parliament. As vicegerent to Henry himself, Cromwell was well placed to guarantee Crown control - he even ranked above the bishops in the Convocation. Such intriguing protocol was itself related to the role of imperial officials at some of the early ecumenical councils. Though he could hardly have welcomed parliamentary sovereignty, Cranmer evidently agreed to uphold a Royal Supremacy which he viewed in precise scriptural terms. In the same way his use of the early Fathers and councils had strengthened his adherence to the Lutheran doctrine of the 'godly prince'. For Cranmer, moreover, this was no sudden Damascus-road enlightenment but his opportunity as archbishop to authenticate in terms of pastoral practice the rejection he felt for papal law and supremacy even in his Cambridge days. When the pulpit was used to rally the parishes to Royal Supremacy, Cranmer readily obeyed the royal mandate, preaching at Canterbury (1535) against what he termed the 'false and unjust usurpation' of 'the bishop of Rome'. Deference made the archbishop send the king a summary of his exposition, 'though my two sermons were long'. It is an interesting letter, and entirely characteristic of the way Cranmer did his best to clear almost everything with Cromwell or the king [**Extract 5**].

If Henry was Supreme Head of the Church, Cranmer was supremely Henry's archbishop; and there is an almost manic quality about the loyal service he rendered his prince. Second only to his concern for the gospel itself, Cranmer revered the doctrine of the 'godly prince'; without it, and without the repudiation of papal supremacy involved, reform of the English Church could scarely have been a live option. Yet 'Supreme Headship' challenged Canterbury's traditional authority at every level, Gardiner scoring a palpable hit in 1535 when he made clear his view that, under new dispensations, Cranmer's archiepiscopal style stood in 'derogation and prejudice of the King's high power and authority, [Henry] being supreme head of the Church'. Unperturbed, Cranmer was convinced that the primate, and those who were genuinely his brother bishops, should 'leave all our styles . . . calling ourselves *apostolos Jesu Christi*'; the claims of pastoral ministry weighed more heavily on him than concern over legal niceties. As Henry's archbishop he knew his duty, and, granted Cromwell's new role, he knew the responsibilities he owed the King's vicegerent, vicar-general and special commissary. In the words of Professor A.G. Dickens, such powers enabled Cromwell:

> to appoint deputy-commissioners at will, give him and them power to visit all ecclesiastical institutions, and make enquiry concerning the conduct of the clergy, 'even if they shine in archi-episcopal or episcopal splendours'. They might punish the culpable by deprivations, suspension or sequestration, control all synods, chapters and convocations, preside over the elections of prelates, cite and coerce all subjects of the realm in causes ecclesiastical, receive the surrender of churches, and in general exercise the full plenitude of ecclesiastical power.

Thomas Cromwell and the English Reformation (London, 1959), p. 124.

That Cromwell in fact exercised precisely this sway, to beat the archbishop at what was, after all, the primate's own game, is apparent from entries in his court book between October 1535 and February 1540. Cranmer received a licence under the Crown, 'at the King's pleasure only', to institute, deprive and collate clergy to livings, to prove wills in his Canterbury court, and to deal with complaints or appeals and such other matters as arose in the day-to-day running of his diocese. But whatever his own pastoral insight and understanding of his authority, the revised wording of a licence that originally began: 'THOMAS permissione divina Cant' archiepiscopus, totius Anglie primas et apostolice sedis legatus natus', henceforth gave Cranmer jurisdictional authority 'by the grace of God' and at the royal pleasure. Dr Paul Ayris is clear that 'Cromwell used his office ... with skill and insight' to wield 'important powers which forged a new relationship between church and state during the years of his ascendancy'.

The fact that Cranmer both co-operated with Cromwell and played his own unique role as archbishop prevented any worsening of Church - State relations under Henry. He even supported the vicegerent in doctrinal matters, although passages in both the *Ten Articles* (1536) and the *Bishops' Book* (1537), suggest that if Cromwell wanted a statement of faith for Henry's Church, Cranmer would do what he could to ensure that some measure of Lutheran tonic was added to a traditional distillation. Diplomatically it was, of course, a time when Cromwell sought support from the Lutheran princes. But even if German confessions like Augsburg (1530) and the *Wittenberg Articles* only surfaced in political debate, they later exercised a theological influence linked to the progress of reformation. There are interesting parallels between the *Wittenberg Articles* (1536) and the English *Ten Articles* of the same year, both acknowledging the bible and the three sacraments of the gospel (baptism, the altar and penance) as true standards of the faith. When treating of justification too, the discussion in the *Ten Articles* shows indisputable traces of *justificatio sola fide* from the Wittenberg formulary, whilst the Eucharist is treated with a caution that altogether avoids the traditional language of sacrifice and scholastic definition of the presence. As for the seven sacraments, the *Bishops' Book* (1537), by enumerating baptism, the altar and penance as 'Sacraments of the Gospel', recognised them as instituted of Christ in a way that the four remaining 'rites' (confirmation, extreme unction, matrimony and even order) were not. No wonder Cranmer had difficulty with 'other bishops and learned men' in what he quaintly termed their 'determination' in the matter; but even the proximity of plague to Lambeth did not prevent him sending a punctilious report to Cromwell, one which included the all too human plea that, in high summer, 'we may have his grace's licence to depart' [**Extract 6**].

Later that same year (1537), in another letter to Cromwell, Cranmer recorded plans for the highest achievement of the partnership, the authorisation and publication of an English bible [**Extract 7**]. Despite many obstacles from traditionalists at home and inquisitors abroad, the vicegerent was as sympathetic to scripture as Cranmer himself, and just as determined to authenticate the 'godly prince' from the very word of God. In this sense the Great Bible (1539), the second edition of which (1540) contained Cranmer's own preface, is as significant a part of Cromwell's legacy as his administrative achievements. The bible's illustrated title-page is certainly an enduring memorial to co-operation between vicegerent and archbishop, as well as a clever way of confronting the reader with Tudor propaganda. For here, enthroned in majesty, the 'godly prince' bestows the very Word of God on both Cromwell and Cranmer who, to the accompaniment of a grateful populace and cries of '*Vivat Rex*' and 'God Save the King', in their turn distribute the scriptures to Henry's subjects.

De temps en temps the prince was not so godly, and that placed his archbishop in desperate straits - in particular there were the crises of 1536 and 1540 when first Anne Boleyn and then Cromwell himself were found guilty of treason. The charge that felled the queen was certainly also a body blow to Cranmer and presented him with one of the cruellest dilemmas of his life. Reformation - a cause that Anne's latest biographer (Eric Ives) notes had received 'a thousand days of support . . . from the throne itself ' - was in jeopardy. With all access to Henry denied, Cranmer had to pen a letter that if it publicly respected the royal charge, nevertheless spelt out boldly and at length the love the queen bore 'towards God and his gospel', to indicate the primate's private doubts about the charge [**Extract 8**]. Cromwell's attainder did not jar his sensitivities in quite the same way, but it undoubtedly saddened Cranmer, who showed courage in standing by his Council colleague. When others shunned the fallen Earl of Essex as 'a most false and corrupt traitor, deceiver and circumventor' against Henry, Cranmer chose to inform the king that he 'loved him as my friend' and that chiefly 'for the love which I thought I saw him bear ever towards your Grace, singularly above all other' [**Extract 9**].

This is not the place to discuss dealings Cranmer had with More and Fisher, Frith and Lambert, let alone to examine the complexities in the case of Queen Catherine Howard (1542) which many writers argue compromised him most of all. Suffice it to state, therefore, that in a period when an archiepiscopal presence remained a fact of court life, whatever the intrigues and opportunism of king and statesmen, there is a genuine consistency in Cranmer's dealings with all sorts and conditions of men that relates to his conviction that, under God, he had a solemn obligation as archbishop to be obedient to the 'godly prince'. For Cranmer indeed, obedience in earthly affairs constituted a spiritual duty. So much is clear from the great *Commonplaces* in both theology and the canon law. Together with immense reserves of patience, such principles alone made his hazardous pilgrimage through Henry VIII's regime possible, just as they brought prince and prelate a special relationship and affection for one another. Nevertheless there is a sense in which the accession of Edward brought Thomas Cranmer a long-awaited reward. For his 'excellent speech' (Strype) at the coronation on 20 February 1547 was both as fulsome in its praise and thanksgiving, as it was fervent in commendation of the doctrine vindicated by the accession 'of a perfect monarch' free from 'tyranny of the bishops of Rome'. Reminding the boy that God gave him a spiritual sword, Cranmer counselled Edward VI to rule like 'a second Josiah' who in his days 'reformed the church of God' [**Extract 10**]. Doubtless uplifted by accession of the young king in much the same way as Luther was heartened in his cause by John Frederick's unquestioning commitment to reformation, Cranmer had yet to deal with Somerset, and with that marionette manipulator, John Dudley.

Extract 1
Cranmer's Protestation
In the name of God, Amen. Before you in my own person and with reliable witnesses here present I, Thomas, Archbishop of Canterbury, elect, say, assert and in this document openly, pubicly and expressly claim: That, although I ought, before my consecration or on that occasion, to take the oath or oaths which are customarily taken to the Supreme Pontiff by those elected to be Archbishops of Canterbury, for form's sake rather than in reality or as a necessary condition of receiving consecration, it is not nor will it be any part of my wish or intention by an oath or oaths of this kind, however the words they contain seem to sound, to bind myself on their account henceforward to say, do or attempt anything which will or may seem to be contrary to God's law, or against His Majesty the King of England, or the state of this his realm of England, or his laws and

prerogatives. And that I do not intend by an oath or oaths of this kind so to bind myself in any way, that I may not be able freely to speak about, debate and agree to in all particulars the reformation of the Christian religion, the government of the English Church, or the prerogatives of the same Crown, or the advantage of the state, to those who are in any way concerned, and everywhere to carry out and reform those things in the English Church which may seem to me to need to be reformed. And I assert and profess that I will take the said oaths in accordance with this interpretation and this understanding and not otherwise nor in any other manner. Moreover I state that whatever oath my Procurator has heretofore taken to the Supreme Pontiff in my name, it was no part of my intention or wish to confer on him any power, by virtue of which he could take any oath in my name contrary or repugnant to the oath taken, or hereafter to be taken, by me to His aforesaid Majesty the King of England. And in the event that he has taken in my name any such contrary or repugnant oath, I state that he has done so without my knowledge and without my authority, and I desire this to be null and void. I desire these protestations to be repeated and reiterated in all the clauses and paragraphs of the said oaths. I do not intend to depart from these protestations by any word or deed of mine, nor shall I so depart; but I wish them to be always kept by me.

Consecration Oath

I, Thomas, Elect of Canterbury from his hour as previously will be faithful and obedient to Blessed Peter, the Holy Apostolic Roman Church, and to my lord, Lord Clement VII, and to his canonically appointed successors. I will not take counsel, consent or do anything to cause them to lose life or limb or be arrested. Any matter they may personally or by envoys entrust to me I will not knowingly disclose to anyone to their detriment. I will be their helper in retaining and defending the Roman Papacy and the regalia of St Peter against all persons, saving my order. I will accord honourable treatment and assistance with necessitites to the Legate of the Apostolic See in coming and returning. When summoned to a synod I will come, unless prevented by a canonical impediment. I will visit the thresholds of the Apostles within the ambit of the Roman Curia this side of the Alps every year, but beyond the mountains every two years, either in person or by my envoy, unless absolved by Apostolic permission. The possessions pertaining to my archiepiscopal household I will not sell, nor give away, nor pledge, nor enfeoff anew, nor in any way alienate, without consulting the Roman Pontiff. So help me God and these holy gospels of God.

Cranmer's protestation and oath can be found in the original Latin as items (Num. V and Num. VI) in the appendix to John Strype, *Memorials of Thomas Cranmer* (London, 1694), pp. 9-10.

Extract 2

I, Thomas Cranmer, renounce and utterly forsake all such clauses, words, sentences, and grants, which I have of the pope's holiness in his bulls of the archbishoprick of Canterbury, that in any manner was, is, or may be hurtful, or prejudicial to your highness, your heirs, successors, estate, or dignity royal: knowledging myself to take and hold the said archbishoprick immediately, and only, of your highness, and of none other. Most lowly beseeching the same for restitution of the temporalities of the said archbishoprick; promising to be faithful, true, and obedient subject to your said highness, your heirs and successors, during my life. So help me God and the holy evangelists!

Cranmer's oath to the king for his temporalties; in *Cranmer II*, p. 460.

Extract 3

I ... am ... most humblie to beseche Your most noble Grace, that wher the office and duetie of thArchbisshop of Canturbery, by your and your progenitours sufferaunce and grauntes, is to directe ordre judge, and determyn causes spirituall, in this Your Graces realme ... it may please therfore, Your most excellent Majestie (considerations had to the premisses, and to my moost bounden duetie towardes Your Hieghnes, your realme, succession, and posterite, and for thexoneration of my conscience towardes Almightie God) to licence me, according to myn office and duetie, to procede to the examination, fynall determynation, and judgement in the said grete cause, touching Your Hieghnes. Eftsones, as prostrate at the feete of Your Majestie, beseching the same to pardone me of thes my bolde and rude letters, and the same to accept and take in good sense and parte, as I do meane; which calling Our Lorde to recorde, is onlie for the zele that I have to the causes aforesaide, and for none other intent and purpose.

Cranmer to Henry VIII, 11 April 1533; in *L & P*, Vol. VI, p. 327. This is the final form approved by the king.

Extract 4

The Thursday next before the feast of Pentecost, the king and the queen being at Greenwich, all the crafts of London thereunto well appointed, in several barges decked after the most gorgeous and sumptuous manner, with divers pageants thereunto belonging, repaired and waited all together upon the mayor of London; and so well furnished came all unto Greenwich, where they tarried and waited for the queen's coming to her barge: which so done, they brought her unto the Tower, trumpets, shambes, and other divers instruments all the way playing and making great melody, which, as is reported, was so comely done as never was like in any time nigh to our remembrance.

And so her grace came to the Tower on Thursday at night, about five of the clock, where also was such a peal of guns as hath not been heard like a great while before. And the same night, and Friday all day, the king and queen tarried there; and on Friday at night the king's grace made eighteen knights of the Bath, whose creation was not alonely so strange to hear of, as also their garments stranger to behold or look on, which said knights the next day, which was Saturday, rid before the queen's grace throughout the city of London towards Westminster palace, over and besides the most part of the nobles of the realm, which like accompanied her grace throughout the said city; she sitting in her hair upon a horse litter, richly apparelled, and four knights of the five ports bearing a canopy over her head. And after her came four rich chariots, one of them empty, and three other furnished with divers ancient old ladies; and after them came a great train of other ladies and gentlewomen: which said progress, from the beginning to the ending, extended half a mile in length by estimation, or thereabout. To whom also, as she came along the city, was shewed many costly pageants, with divers other encomies spoken of children to her. Wine also running at certain conduits plentifully. And so proceeding throughout the streets, passed forth unto Westminster-hall, where was a certain banquet prepared for her; which done, she was conveyed out of the backside of the palace into a barge, and so unto York-place, where the king's grace was before her coming: for this you must ever presuppose, that his grace came always before her secretly in a barge, as well from Greenwich to the Tower, as from the Tower to York-place.

Now then on Sunday was the coronation, which also was of such a manner. In the morning there assembled with me at Westminster church the bishop of York, the bishop of London, the bishop of Winchester, the bishop of Lincoln, the bishop of Bath, and the bishop of St Asse; the abbot of Westminster, with ten or twelve more abbots; which all revestred ourselves in our pontificalibus, and so furnished, with our crosses and crosiers, proceeded out of the abbey in a procession unto Westminster-hall, where we received the queen apparelled in a robe of purple velvet, and all the ladies and gentle-women in robes and gowns of scarlet, according to the manner used before time in such business: and so her grace sustained of each side with two bishops, the bishop of London and the bishop of Winchester, came forth in procession unto the church of Westminster, she in her hair, my lord of Suffolk bearing before her the crown, and two other lords bearing also before her a sceptre and a white rod, and so entered up into the high altar, where divers ceremonies used about her, I did set the crown on her head, and then was sung *Te Deum*, &c. And after that was sung a solemn mass: all which while her grace sat crowned upon a scaffold, which was made between the high altar and the choir in Westminster church; which mass and ceremonies done and finished, all the assembly of noblemen brought her into Westminster-hall again, where was kept a great solemn feast all that day; the good order thereof were too long to write at this time to you. But now, sir, you may not imagine that this coronation was before her marriage; for she was married much about St Paul's day last, as the condition thereof doth well appear, by reason she is now somewhat big with child. Notwith-standing it hath been reported throughout a great part of the realm that I married her; which was plainly false, for I myself knew not thereof a fortnight after it was done. And many other things be also reported of me, which be mere lies and tales.

Cranmer to Archdeacon Hawkins, from Croydon, 17 June 1533; in *Cranmer II*, pp. 245-6.

Extract 5

Pleaseth it your grace to be advertised, that where, as well by your grace's special letters, dated the third day of June in the xxviith year of your grace's most noble reign, as also by mouth in Winchester at Michaelmas last past, your grace commanded all the prelates of your realm, that they will all acceleration and expedition should do their diligence every one in his diocese, fully to persuade your people of the bishop of Rome his authority, that it is but a false and unjust usurpation, and that your grace, of very right and by God's law, is the supreme head of this church of England, next immediately unto God; I, to accomplish your grace's commandment, incontinent upon my return from Winchester (knowing that all the country about Otford and Knoll, where my most abode was, were sufficiently instructed in those matters already), came up into these parts of East Kent, only by preaching to persuade the people in the said two articles: and in mine own church at Canterbury, because I was informed that that town in those two points was least persuaded of all my diocese, I preached there two sermons myself; and, as it then chanced, Dr Leighton was present at my first sermon, being then your grace's visitor. Of whom, if it so please your grace, you may hear the report, what I preached.

The scope and effect of both my sermons stood in three things. First, I declared that the bishop of Rome was not God's vicar in earth, as he was taken: and although it was so taught these three or four hundreth years, yet it was done by means of the bishop of Rome, who compelled men by oaths so to teach, to the maintenance of his authority, contrary to God's word. And here I declared by what means and craft the bishops of Rome obtained such usurped authority.

Second, because the see of Rome was called 'sancta sedes Romana,' and the bishop was called 'sanctissimus papa,' and men's consciences peradventure could not be quiet to be separated from so holy a place, and from God's most holy vicar; I shewed the people that this thing ought nothing to move them, for it was but a holiness in name; for indeed there was no such holiness at Rome. And hereupon I took occasion to declare the glory and pomp of Rome, the covetousness, the unchaste living, and the maintenance of all vices.

Third, I spake against the bishop of Rome his laws; which he calleth 'divinas leges,' and 'sacros canones,' and maketh them equal with God's law. And here I declared that many of his laws were contrary to God's laws. And some of them which were good and laudable, yet they were not of such holiness as he would make them; that is, to be taken as God's laws, or to have remission of sins by observing of them. And here I said, that so many of his laws as were good, men ought not to contemn and despise them, and wilfully to break them; for those that be good your grace had received as laws of your realm, until such time as others should be made. And therefore as laws of your realm they must be observed, and not contemned.

And here I spake as well of the ceremonies of the church . . . that they ought neither to be rejected or despised, nor yet to be observed with this opinion, that they of themselves make men holy, or that they remit sin. For seeing that our sins be remitted by the death of our

Saviour Christ Jesus, I said it was too much injury to Christ to impute the remission of our sins to any laws or ceremonies of man's making: nor the laws and ceremonies of the church at their first making were ordained for that intent. But as the common laws of your grace's realm be not made to remit sin, nor no man doth observe them for that intent, but for a common commodity, and for a good order and quietness to be observed among your subjects; even so were the laws and ceremonies first instituted in the church for a good order...

Though my two sermons were long, yet I have written briefly unto your highness the sum of them both. And I was informed by sundry reports, that the people were glad that they heard so much as they did; ...

I beseech your grace to pardon me of my long and tedious writing; for I could not otherwise set the matter forth plain. And I most heartily thank your grace for the stag which your grace sent unto me from Windsor forest: which, if your grace knew for how many causes it was welcome unto me, and how many ways it did me service, I am sure you would think it much the better bestowed. Thus our Lord have your highness always in his preservation and governance.

Cranmer to Henry VIII, from Ford, 26 August 1536; in *Cranmer II*, pp. 325-8.

Extract 6

After most hearty commendations unto your lordship: these shall be to signify unto you, that I, with other bishops and learned men here assembled by the king's commandment, have almost made an end of our determinations: for we have already subscribed unto the declarations of the Pasternoster and the Ave Maria, the creed and the ten commandments; and there remainth no more but certain notes of the creed, unto the which we be agreed to subscribe on Monday next: which all, when they shall be subscribed, I pray you that I may know your mind and pleasure, whether I shall send them incontinently unto you, or leave them in my lord of Herteforde's hands, to be delivered by him when he cometh next unto the court: beseeching you, my lord, to be intercessor unto the king's highness for us all, that we may have his grace's licence to depart for this time, until his grace's further pleasure be known; for they die almost every where in London, Westminster, and in Lambeth they die at my gate even at the next house to me. I would fain see the king's highness at my departing, but I fear me that I shall not, by cause that I shall come from this smoky air; yet I

would gladly know the king's pleasure herein.
Cranmer to Cromwell, from Lambeth, 21 July 1537; in *Cranmer II*, pp. 337-8.

Extract 7

My very singular and especial good lord, in my most hearty wise I commend me to your lordship. These shall be to give you most hearty thanks that any heart can think, and that in the name of them all which favoureth God's word, for your diligence at this time in procuring the king's highness to set forth the said God's word and his gospel by his grace's authority. For the which act, not only the king's majesty, but also you shall have a perpetual laud and memory of all them that be now, or hereafter shall be, God's faithful people and the favourers of his word. And this deed you shall hear of at the great day, when all things shall be opened and made manifest. For our Saviour Christ saith in the said gospel, that whosoever shrinketh from him and his word, and is abashed to profess and set it forth before men in this world, he will refuse him at that day; and contrary, whosoever constantly doth profess him and his word, and studieth to set that forward in this world, Christ will declare the same at the last day before his Father and all his angels, and take upon him the defence of those men.
Cranmer to Cromwell, from Ford, 28 August 1537; in *Cranmer II*, pp. 346-7.

Extract 8

Pleaseth it your most noble grace to be advertised, that at your grace's commandment by Mr Secretary his letters written in your grace's name, I came to Lamehith yesterday, and do there remain to know your grace's further pleasure. And forsomuch as without your grace's commandment I dare not, contrary to the contents of the said letters, presume to come unto your grace's presence; nevertheless of my most bounden duty, I can do no less than most humbly to desire your grace, by your great wisdom and by the assistance of God's help, somewhat to suppress the deep sorrows of your grace's heart, and to take all adversities of God's hand both patiently and thankfully.

I cannot deny but your grace hath great causes many ways of lamentable heaviness; and also, that in the wrongful estimation of the world your grace's honour of every part is so highly touched (whether the things that commonly be spoken of be true, or not), that I remember not that ever Almighty God sent unto your grace any like occasion to try your grace's constancy throughout, whether your highness can be content to take of God's hand as well things displeasant as pleasant.

And if he find in your noble heart such an obedience unto his will, that your grace, without murmuration and overmuch heaviness, do accept all adversities, not less thanking him than when all things succeeded after your grace's will and pleasure, nor less procuring his glory and honour; then I suppose your grace did never thing more acceptable unto him, since your first governance of this your realm: and moreover, your grace shall give unto him occasion to multiply and increase his graces and benefits unto your highness, as he did unto his most faithful servant Job; unto whom, after his great calamities and heaviness, for his obedient heart and willing acceptation of God's scourge and rod, '*addidit ei Dominus cuncta duplicia*'.

And if it be true, that is openly reported of the queen's grace; if men had a right estimation of things, they should not esteem any part of your grace's honour to be touched thereby, but her honour only to be clearly disparaged. And I am in such a perplexity, that my mind is clean amazed; for I never had better opinion in woman than I had in her; which maketh me to think, that she should not be culpable. And again, I think your highness would not have gone so far, except she had surely been culpable. Now I think that your grace best knoweth, that next unto your grace I was most bound unto her of all creatures living. Wherefore I most humbly beseech your grace to suffer me in that, which both God's law, nature, and also her kindness, bindeth me unto; that is, that I may with your grace's favour wish and pray for her, that she may declare herself inculpable and innocent. And if she be found culpable, considering your grace's goodness towards her, and from what condition your grace of your only mere goodness took her and set the crown upon her head; I repute him not your grace's faithful servant and subject, nor true unto the realm, that would not desire the offence without mercy to be punished to the example of all other. And as I loved her not a little for the love which I judged her to bear towards God and his gospel; so, if she be proved culpable, there is not one that loveth God and his gospel that ever will favour her, but must hate her above all other; and the more they favour the gospel, the more they will hate her: for then there was never creature in our time that so much slandered the gospel; and God hath sent her this punishment, for that she feignedly hath professed his gospel in her mouth, and not in heart and deed.

And though she have offended so, that she hath deserved never to be reconciled unto your grace's favour; yet Almighty God hath manifoldly declared his goodness towards your grace, and never

offended you. But your grace, I am sure, knowledgeth that you have offended him. Wherefore I trust that your grace will bear no less entire favour unto the truth of the gospel, than you did before; forsomuch as your grace's favour to the gospel was not led by affection unto her, but by zeal unto the truth. And thus I beseech Almighty God, whose gospel he hath ordained your grace to be defender of, ever to preserve your grace from all evil, and give you at the end the promise of his gospel.
Cranmer to Henry VIII, from Lambeth, 3 May 1536; in *Cranmer II*, pp. 323-4.

Extract 9

I heard yesterday in your grace's council, that he [Cromwell] is a traitor: yet who cannot be sorrowful and amazed that he should be a traitor against your majesty, he that was so advanced by your majesty; he whose surety was only by your majesty; he who loved your majesty (as I ever thought) no less than God; he who studied always to set forwards whatsoever was your majesty's will and pleasure; he that cared for no man's displeasure to serve your majesty; he that was such a servant, in my judgment, in wisdom, diligence, faithfulness, and experience as no prince in this realm ever had; he that was so vigilant to preserve your majesty from all treasons, that few could be so secretly conceived, but he detected the same in the beginning? If the noble princes of memory, king John, Henry the second, and Richard II, had had such a councillor about them, I suppose that they should never have been so traitorously abandoned and overthrown as those good princes were .... I loved him as my friend, for so I took him to be; but I chiefly loved him for the love which I thought I saw him bear ever towards your grace, singularly above all other. But now, if he be a traitor, I am sorry that ever I loved him or trusted him, and I am very glad that his treason is discovered in time: but yet again I am very sorrowful; for who shall your grace trust hereafter, if you might not trust him? Alas! I bewail and lament your grace's chance herein, I wot not whom your grace may trust. But I pray God continually night and day, to send such a counsellor in his place whom your grace may trust, and who for all his qualities can and will serve your grace like to him, and that will have so much solicitude and care to preserve your grace from all dangers as I ever thought he had. . .
Cranmer to Henry VIII; in *Cranmer II*, p. 401.

Extract 10

Most dread and royal sovereign: The promises your highness hath made here at your coronation, to forsake the devil and all his works, are not to be taken in the bishop of Rome's sense, when you commit any thing distasteful to that see, to hit your majesty in the teeth; as pope Paul the third, late bishop of Rome, sent to your royal father, saying, 'Didst thou not promise, at our permission of thy coronation, to forsake the devil and all his works, and dost thou turn to heresy? For the breach of this thy promise, knowest thou not, that 'tis in our power to dispose of the sword and sceptre to whom we please?' We, your majesty's clergy, do humbly conceive, that this promise reacheth not at your highness' sword, spiritual or temporal, or in the least at your highness swaying the sceptre of this your dominion, as you and your predecessors have had them from God. . . .

The bishops of Canterbury for the most part have crowned your predecessors, and anointed them kings of this land: yet it was not in their power to receive or reject them, neither did it give them authority to prescribe them conditions to take or to leave their crowns; although the bishops of Rome would encroach upon your predecessors by his bishops' act and oil, that in the end they might possess those bishops with an interest to dispose of their crowns at their pleasure. But the wiser sort will look to their claws and clip them.

The solemn rites of coronation have their ends and utility, yet neither direct force or necessity: they be good admonitions to put kings in mind of their duty to God, but no increasement of their dignity. For they be God's anointed, not in respect of the oil which the bishop useth, but in consideration of their power which is ordained, of the sword which is authorised, of their persons which are elected by God, and endued with the gifts of his Spirit for the better ruling and guiding of his people. The oil, if added, is but a ceremony; if it be wanting, that king is yet a perfect monarch notwithstanding, and God's anointed, as well as if he was inoiled. . . .

Therefore not from the bishop of Rome, but as a messenger from my Saviour Jesus Christ, I shall most humbly admonish your royal majesty, what things your highness is to perform.

Your majesty is God's vice-gerent and Christ's vicar within your own dominions, and to see, with your predecessor Josiah, God truly worshipped, and idolatry destroyed, the tyranny of the bishops of Rome banished from your subjects, and images removed. These acts be signs of a second Josiah, who reformed the church of God in his days. You are to reward virtue, to revenge sin, to justify the innocent, to relieve the poor, to procure peace, to repress violence, and to execute justice throughout your realms. For precedents, on those kings who performed not these things, the old law shews how the Lord revenged his quarrel; and on those kings who fulfilled these things, he poured forth his blessings in abundance. For example, it is written of Josiah in the book of the Kings thus: 'Like unto him there was no king before him that turned to the Lord with all his heart, according to all the law of Moses, neither after him arose there any like him.' This was to that prince a perpetual fame of dignity, to remain to the end of days.

From Cranmer's address at the Coronation of King Edward VI, 20 February 1547; in *Cranmer II*, pp. 126-7.

4
Word and Worship

When, in the memorable language of the preface (*paraclesis*) to *Novum instrumentum omne*, Erasmus sought to popularise the scriptures, eagerly anticipating the time when 'the countryman might sing them at his plough, the weaver chant them at his loom, the traveller beguile with them the tedium of his journey', the force of his words was such that they soon secured Europe-wide circulation. The task of writing in the vernacular Erasmus left to others; and it was, of course, some time before countrymen and townsfolk could be confronted with the bible in their own language. Echoes of this famous passage are nevertheless to be found in many contemporary writings, Cranmer almost certainly applying the idea of a traveller warding off the weariness of his journey to the Ethiopian eunuch 'occupied with worldy cures and businesses, . . . riding in his chariot . . . reading the Scripture'. The passage comes in his *Preface* to the second edition of the Great Bible (1540). The archbishop made the most of the rare pastoral opportunity the publication presented of commending the 'largeness and utility of the scripture' to his flock [**Extract 1**].

On the continent, renewed interest in the bible and its translation had prompted much controversy. Christian humanists and reforming divines had pleaded the cause of both 'old' and 'new' religions, especially concentrating their minds on the problem of authority. While there was continuing concern to establish an accurate text, much ink also flowed as commentators addressed themselves to the crucial issue of priority. Did the bible derive authority from the Church? Or, as the Swiss in particular urged, was not 'the Christian church . . . born out of the Word of God'? It was study of the scriptures that had compelled the conscience-stricken Luther to make his obdurate stand against papal authority, and *sola scriptura* became by logic and momentum the doctrine of the 'prostestants'.

In England, there is little evidence to suggest that Cranmer was directly concerned by such issues. Rather did Henry's archbishop address himself to second-generation assessments, penning for his province the mature judgements that come when controversy is past. Obliged to proceed with caution, Cranmer in his letters to Cromwell clearly expresses a deep sense of gratitude once royal authority for an approved bible 'to be bought and read within this realm' had been secured. Cromwell's news gave personal satisfaction to the primate who found 'more pleasure herein, than if you had given me a thousand pound'. A fortnight later, still encouraged by the royal proclamation, he wrote again. This letter made much of the role of the Lord Privy Seal, Cromwell, and afforded him full praise for what Cranmer clearly regarded as an achievement of the greatest significance for the nation [**Extract 7, Chapter 3**].

Although far from securing the reform he increasingly desired for the English Church, Cranmer had done much to model Henrician formularies of the faith, such as the *Ten Articles* (1536) and the *Bishops' Book* (1537), on German confessions and articles like those of Augsburg and Wittenberg. His preface to the Great Bible laid down priorities which he observed as far as possible, even after the Catholic party, led by Gardiner, bishop of Winchester, marked its ascendancy with the Act of Six Articles, which compelled caution on those favouring the new religion. Such opposition notwithstanding, the archbishop continued to give priority to scripture as he understood it; even the *King's Book* (1543) contained many passages that, although decidedly at variance with doctrinal discussion in the earlier formulary, are nevertheless patient of a reformed understanding. In short, some years before his celebrated liturgical work was produced, it is possible to identify a calculated ambiguity as the hallmark of Cranmer's composition.

When occasion demanded otherwise, however, as in the case of a Kentish JP, Cranmer felt no such inhibitions. He set out in a detailed series of letters for Cromwell to show the king the grievance he felt that a local worthy should object to 'such things as of late years hath been set forth by the authority of the word of God' [**Extract 2**]. Cranmer suggested the justice should study the scripture, but the worthy was confident that, although he was 'meanly learned in morality', it was not his task; and writing from Minster in Thanet he declared he would by no means 'with little learning and less discretion' presume to 'high knowledge, as I see many do now-a-days'. It was a conservative lawyer's shrewd reaction to Cranmer's incautious references to such watchwords of 'new religion' as 'the point of our justification by Christ's passion only' [**Extract 3**].

Although it was still early days, the new regime of Somerset afforded the archbishop full scope for clarity of expression in dealing with the rebellious men of Devon and Cornwall (1549). Cranmer's *Answer* provides the historian with a normative document. The important patristic and conciliar material raised by his discussion of the *Fifteen Articles* has already come under scrutiny. In the present context it remains to discuss the weight Cranmer placed on the availability of scripture in 'the tongue understanded of the people' [**Extract 4**]. His apparent inconsistency in this matter has often made him an object of derision to critics who argue that he should have supplied some kind of Cornish service-book to counter the rebel accusation that his 'new service' was unacceptable and 'like a Christmas game'. The masterly answer he actually gave ought to be more widely known, based as it is on the importance of a biblical base in teaching ministry [**Extract 5**].

To understand the nature of such ministry, worship 'grounded upon the holy scriptures' must itself come under careful scrutiny. For firmly founded in the critical method of the 'new divinity', Cranmer brought into play a hermeneutic that transformed the public services of the 'new religion'. Drafted as early as 1543 when the royal whim wished 'general rogations and processions to be made', Cranmer's letter of 7 October 1544 gave the king a most detailed insight into the way he shaped the English Litany. With many a madrigal to his credit by this advanced date, the Renaissance prince in Henry VIII can only have applauded the balanced grasp of a prelate fully persuaded that 'the song that shall be made thereunto would not be full of notes, but, as near as may be, for every syllable a note' [**Extract 6**]. Although the Litany drew heavily on both medieval processionals and Luther's recent liturgical work, it was essentially biblical in orientation, the last unique suffrage in every way symbolising the first-fruits of his liturgical genius:

That it may please thee to give us true repentance;
to forgive us all our sins, negligences, and ignorances;
and to endue us with the grace of the Holy Spirit, to
amend our lives according to thy holy Word.

Traditional observances were held by some to be superstitious, but Cranmer was no iconoclast bent on removing images overnight and, like Luther's Karlstadt, putting nothing in their place. That same year, the *King's Book*, in the context of the idolatry condemned by the second commandment, had made reference to the popular practice of 'creeping to the cross'. This the archbishop deplored as 'a greater abuse than any ... for there you say, *Crucem tuam adoramus, Domine*; and the ordinal saith, *Procedant clerici ad crucem adorandum nudis pedibus*; and after followeth ... *Ponatur crux ante aliquod altare, ubi a populo adoretur.*' Yet, though he informed Henry that his pleasure was that 'the said creeping to the cross shall ... cease from henceforth and be abolished', Cranmer's understanding of the people's worship would not let him simply leave the matter there [**Extract 7**].

Later (*Common Prayer* will be discussed in Chapter 5), a letter of September 1555, to Mary sustains such insights, Cranmer effectively offering the Queen a lengthy *apologia*, part of which sets out his principled approach to worship of the kind he held had been commended by the apostle Paul, namely, 'praying, singing, lauding, and thanking of God ... whereunto the people say Amen' [**Extract 8**].

Extract 1

Wherefore, in few words to comprehend the largeness and utility of the scripture, how it containeth fruitful instruction and erudition for every man; if any things be necessary to be learned, of the holy scripture we may learn it. If falsehood shall be reproved, thereof we may gather wherewithal. If any thing be to be corrected and amended, if there need any exhortation or consolation, of the scripture we may well learn. In the scriptures be the fat pastures of the soul; therein is no venomous meat, no unwholesome thing; they be the very dainty and pure feeding. He that is ignorant, shall find there what he should learn. He that is a perverse sinner, shall there find his damnation to make him to tremble for fear. He that laboureth to serve God, shall find there his glory, and the promissions of eternal life, exhorting him more diligently to labour. Herein may princes learn how to govern their subjects; subjects obedience, love and dread to their princes: husbands, how they should behave them unto their wives; how to educate their children and servants: and contrary the wives, children, and servants may know their duty to their husbands, parents and masters. Here may all manner of persons, men, women, young, old, learned, unlearned, rich, poor, priests, laymen, lords, ladies, officers, tenants,

and mean men, virgins, wives, widows, lawyers, merchants, artific-
ers, husbandmen, and all manner of persons, of what estate or
condition soever they be, may in this book learn all things what they
ought to believe, what they ought to do, and what they should not
do, as well concerning Almighty God, as also concerning themselves and all other. Briefly, to the reading of the scripture none can
be enemy, but that either be so sick that they love not to hear of any
medicine, or else that be so ignorant that they know not scripture
to be the most healthful medicine.

A Prologue or Preface to the Great Bible, 1540; in *Cranmer II,* p. 121.

Extract 2

... and besides this, it is known to many, that you let, in as much as in
you is, the people in my diocese to exercise themselves in the
knowledge of God's laws; but that from time to time you promote
them to all trouble and vexation, without any discerning good
knowledge from manifest error, so that (as it is thought) you rather
thereby intend to extinguish the whole knowledge of God, than to
have him by his word known and glorified. I pray you, what other
ways was there at any time invented better to maintain, continue,
or uphold the bishop of Rome's usurped authority and other
superstitiousness, than to banish and suppress the word of God and
the knowledge thereof specially from the simple and common
people, and to restrain the same to the knowledge of a certain few
persons? yea, this thing has been universally the only decay of our
faith. And why then may not men think of you to be a special
favourer covertly of his authority, when you bear the people such
a hatred for favouring of God's word, which word hath uttered unto
all the world his crafty inventions?

Cranmer to a Kentish justice, 1537 (written in the hand of one of the archbishop's
secretaries); in *Cranmer II,* p. 350.

Extract 3

And inasmuch as you say that I judged you, before I knew you, not to
be a favourer of God's word, and so doth persist in that opinion, in
manner as if I had so tried you: in that you may perceive that there was
a fame of you in this behalf before I knew you; which declareth that
neither I nor none of mine hath invented any such things against you
of late; and therefore, the fame not yet quenched made me to write my
mind so plainly to you as I did. As for the profession of your religion,

that you love God and his most blessed word, believe in him, dread him, &c. I did never doubt in that behalf at all, but that you had a fervent zeal to him, saving that it may be doubtful whether that zeal were according to knowledge, or no: specially considering that in your sessions and elsewhere you be not so diligent nor circumspect to open and set forth things requisite of necessity to our salvation (as the point of our justification by Christ's passion only, the difference between faith and works, works of mercy to be done before voluntary works, the obedience towards our prince by the authority of the word of God, and such other concerning the stiff opinion of the people in alteration of ordinances and laws in the church, as holidays, fasting days, &c.) as you be in the declaration and setting forth of mere voluntary things, of the which we have no ground ne foundation of scripture.

Cranmer to a Kentish justice, 1537; in *Cranmer II*, p. 353.

Extract 4

But if reason will not persuade you, I will prove what God's word will do unto you. St Paul, in the first epistle to the Corinthians, saith, that whosoever shall speak to the people in the church to their edification, must speak such language as the people may understand; or else he willeth him to hold his peace, and speak softly to himself and to God. For he which speaketh a strange language which the people understand not, doth not edify them, as St Paul saieth. And he giveth an example of the trumpet in the field, which when it giveth such a sound that the soldier understandeth, it availeth much: for every soldier thereby knoweth what to do. But if such a blast be blown as no man understandeth, then the blast is utterly in vain: for no man knoweth thereby, whether the horsemen shall make them ready, or leap upon horseback, or go to their standard; or whether the footmen shall make them ready, or set themselves in array, or set upon the enemy, or retire to the standard. Even so should the priests be God's trump in his church: so that if he blow such a certain blast that the people may understand, they be much edified thereby; but if he give such a sound as is to the people unknown, it is clearly in vain, saith St Paul: for he speaks to the air; but no man is the better or edified thereby, nor knoweth what he should do by that he heareth. Furthermore, in the same place St Paul saieth, that if a man giveth thanks to God in a language to the people unknown, how can they say *Amen* to that they understand not? He doth well in giving thanks to God; but that nothing availeth or edifieth the people, that know not what he saith. And St Paul in one brief sentence concludeth his whole disputation of that matter, saying: 'I had rather have five words spoken in the church to the instruction and edifying of the people, than ten thousand in a language unknown, that edifieth not.' And for this purpose allegeth the prophet Esay, who saith, that 'God will speak to his people in other tongues, and in other languages;' meaning thereby, that he would speak to every country in their own language. So have the Greeks the mass in the Greek tongue, the Syrians in the Syry tongue, the Armenians in their tongue, and the Indians in their own tongue. And be you so much addict to the Romish tongue (which is the Latin tongue) that you will have your mass in one other language but the Romish language? Christ himself used among the Jews the Jews' language, and willed his apostles to do the like in every country wheresoever they came. And be you such enemies to your own country, that you will not suffer us to laud God, to thank him, and to use his sacraments in our own tongue; but will enforce us contrary, as well to all reason, as to the word of God?

Answer to the Fifteen Articles of the Rebels, in *Cranmer II*, p. 170.

Extract 5

It is more like a game and a fond play to be laughed at of all men, to hear the priest speak aloud to the people in Latin, and the people listen with their ears to hear; and some walking up and down in the church, some saying other prayers in Latin, and none understandeth other. Neither the priest nor his parish wot what they say. And many times the thing that the priest saith in Latin is so fond of itself, that it is more like a play than a godly prayer.

But in the English service appointed to be read there is nothing else but the eternal word of God: the new and the old Testament is read, that hath power to save your souls; which, as St Paul saith, 'is the power of God to the salvation of all that believe;' the clear light to our eyes, without the which we cannot see; and a lantern unto our feet, without which we should stumble in darkness. It is in itself the wisdom of God, and yet 'to the Jews it is a stumblingblock, and to the Gentiles it is but foolishness: but to such as be called of God, whether they be Jews or Gentiles, it is the power of God, and the wisdom of God.' Then unto you if it be but foolishness and a Christmas game, you may discern yourselves what miserable state you be in, and how far you be from God. For St Paul saith plainly, that the word of God is foolishness only to them that perish; but to them that shall be saved it is God's might and power. . . .

But forasmuch as you understand not the old Latin service, I shall rehearse some things in English that were wont to be read in Latin, that when you understand them, you may judge them whether they seem to be true tales, or fables; and whether they or God's word seem to be more like plays and Christmas games. 'The devil entered into a certain person, in whose mouth St Martin put his finger; and because the devil could not get out at his mouth, the man blew him out behind.' This is one of the tales that was wont to be read in the Latin service, that you will needs have again. As though the devil had a body, and that so crass that he could not pass out by the small pores of the flesh, but must needs have a wide hole to go out at. Is this a grave and godly matter to be read in the church, or rather a foolish Christmas tale, or an old wives' fable, worthy to be laughed at and scorned of every man that hath either wit or godly judgement? Yet more foolish, erroneous, and superstitious things be read in the feasts of St Blase, St Valentine, St Margaret, St Peter, of the Visitation of Our Lady, and the Conception, of the Transfiguration of Christ, and in the feast of Corpus Christi, and a more number mo: whereof some be most vain fables, some very superstitious, some directly against God's word, and the laws of this realm; and all together be full of error and superstition.

Answer to the Fifteen Articles of the Rebels; in Cranmer II, p. 180-1.

Extract 6

It may please your majesty to be advertised, that according to your highness' commandment, sent unto me by your grace's secretary, Mr Pagett, I have translated into the English tongue, so well as I could in so short time, certain processions, to be used upon festival days, if after due correction and amendment of the same your highness shall think it so convenient. In which translation, forasmuch as many of the processions, in the Latin, were but barren, as meseemed, and little fruitful, I was constrained to use more than the liberty of a translator: for in some processions I have altered divers words; in some I have added part; in some taken part away; some I have left out whole, either for by cause the matter appeared to me to be little to purpose, or by cause the days be not with us festival-days; and some processions I have added whole, because I thought I had better matter for the purpose, than was the procession in Latin: the judgement whereof I refer wholly unto your majesty; and after your highness hath corrected it, if your grace command some devout and solemn note to be made thereunto (as is to the procession which your majesty hath already set forth in English), I trust it will much excitate and stir the hearts of all men unto devotion and godliness: but in mine opinion, the song that shall be made thereunto would not be full of notes, but, as near as may be, for every syllable a note; so that it may be sung distinctly and devoutly, as be in the Matins and Evensong, *Venite*, the Hymns, *Te Deum, Benedictus, Magnificat, Nunc dimittis*, and all the Psalms and Versicles; and in the mass *Gloria in Excelsis, Gloria Patri*, the Creed, the Preface, the *Pater noster*, and some of the *Sanctus* and *Agnus*. As concerning the *Salve festa dies*, the Latin note, as I think, is sober and distinct enough; wherefore I have travailed to make the verses in English, and have put the Latin note unto the same. Nevertheless they that be cunning in singing can make a much more solemn note thereto. I made them only for a proof, to see how English would do in song. But by cause mine English verses lack the grace and facility that I would wish they had, your majesty may cause some other to make them again, that can do the same in more pleasant English and phrase.

Cranmer to King Henry VIII, from Bekesbourne, 7 October 1544; in *Cranmer II*, p. 412.

Extract 7

... in my opinion, when such things be altered or taken away, there would be set forth some doctrine therewith, which should declare the cause of the abolishing or alteration, for to satisfy the conscience of the people: for if the honouring of the cross, as creeping and kneeling thereunto, be taken away, it shall seem to many that be ignorant, that the honour of Christ is taken away, unless some good teaching be set forth withal to instruct them sufficiently therein. . . .

Cranmer to King Henry VIII, from Bekesbourne, 24 January 1546; in *Cranmer II*, p. 415.

Extract 8

... whereas by God's laws all christian people be bounden diligently to learn his word, that they may know how to believe and live accordingly, for that purpose he ordained holy days, when they ought, leaving apart all other business, to give themselves wholly to know and serve God. Therefore God's will and commandment is, that when the people be gathered together, ministers should use such language as the people may understand and take profit thereby, or else hold their peace. For as an harp or lute, if it give no certain sound, that men may know what is stricken, who can dance after it? for all the sound is in vain: so is it vain and profiteth nothing, saith Almighty God by the mouth of St Paul, if the priest speak to the people in a language which they know not; 'for else he may profit himself, but profiteth not the people', saith St Paul. But herein I was answered thus; that St Paul spake only of preaching, that the preacher should preach in a tongue which the people did know, or else his preaching availeth nothing... But if the preaching availeth nothing, being spoken in a language which the people understand not, how should any other service avail them, being spoken in the same language? And yet that St Paul meant not only of preaching, it appeareth plainly by his own words. For he speaketh by name expressly of praying, singing, lauding, and thanking of God, and of all other things which the priests say in the churches, whereunto the people say Amen; which they used not in preaching, but in other divine service: that whether the priests rehearse the wonderful works of God, or the great benefits of God unto mankind above all other creatures, or give thanks unto God, or make open profession of their faith, or humble confession of their sins, with earnest request of mercy and forgiveness, or make suit or request unto God for any thing; that then all the people understanding what the priests say, might give their minds and voices with them, and say Amen, that is to say, allow what the priests say; that the rehearsal of God's universal works and benefits, the giving of thanks, the profession of faith, the confession of sins, and the requests and petitions of the priests and the people might ascend up into the ears of God all together, and be as a sweet savour, odour, and incense in his nose: and thus it was used many hundred years after Christ's ascension. But the aforesaid things cannot be done, when the priests speak to the people in a language not known; and so they (or their clerk in their name) say Amen, but they cannot tell where unto. Wheras St Paul saith, 'How can the people say Amen to thy well saying, when they understand not what thou sayest?' And thus was St Paul understanden of all interpreters, both the Greeks and Latins, old and new, school-authors and others, that I have read, until about thirty years past: at which time one Eckius, with other of his sort, began to devise a new exposition, understanding St Paul of preaching only.

But when a good number of the best learned men reputed within this realm, some favouring the old, some the new learning, as they term it (where indeed that which they call the old is the new, and that

which they call the new is indeed the old), but when a great number of
such learned men of both sorts were gathered together at Windsor, for
the reformation of the service of the church; it was agreed by both,
without controversy (not one saying the contrary), that the service of
the church ought to be in the mother-tongue, and that St Paul in the
fourteenth chapter to the Corinthians was so to be understanden.

Cranmer to Queen Mary, September 1555; in *Cranmer II*, p. 450.

5
Common Prayer

The word 'incomparable' is repeatedly used to describe Thomas Cranmer's liturgical achievement. Yet to judge from endless disputes about the origins and content of the English services for which the Tudor primate was largely responsible, a word like 'indescribable' could equally have done duty in so far as few who have judged Cranmer have managed to grasp the full measure of his genius. In fact, given his grounding in the new learning, and the genuine grasp of scripture and 'the ancient authors' that this gave him, the task that faced Cranmer was essentially one of communication - the pastor's perennial problem of inspiring his people to worship their God. The critical studies of Erasmus and a whole band of Christian humanists had made their philological impact to revise the meaning of much traditional vocabulary. And from the standpoint of this 'New Divinity', Cranmer, with his concern for soundness in doctrine and the orderly life, was to mould what Tudor contemporaries termed 'the new religion'.

During his childhood at Aslockton, and in his Cambridge period, Cranmer became increasingly familiar with the Mass, that most significant act of sacramental worship in the Western Church. At Cambridge he would have been aware of the crucial questions raised by Erasmus and the mounting debate in donnish circles. Published in 1516, Erasmus's *Novum instrumentum* - rather than the emerging heresy of a certain Martin Luther - would have been subjected to the scrutiny of *habitués* of the White Horse Inn across the road from Corpus Christi between King's and St Catharine's Colleges. In 1518, this new approach was much strengthened by the appearance, as a separate tract, of the guidelines Erasmus had laid down after the *paraclesis* of his *magnum opus*. This was the *Ratio verae theologiae*, which stressed the importance of studying the New Testament in the original languages, and of bringing all branches of the humanities - philosophy, history, geography and mythology, as well as classical literature and languages - to bear upon it. Erasmus wrote:

We may follow the story, and seem not only to read it but to see it; for it is wonderful how much light - how much life, so to state - is thrown by this method into what before seemed dry and lifeless.

The argument was that faith in the Christian religion should be vested in its own sources and the dogmatism of ecclesiastical authority confronted with the New Testament evidence. It was clearly a development that sent scholars scurrying back to the sources, and the period witnessed a mounting and determined clamour for scriptural translation which was closer to the original text than the often careless renderings in the Latin text of Jerome's long-serving Vulgate (which went back to 404). Compelling questions confronted both the Church hierarchy and university philosophers as legalism and scholasticism were increasingly challenged by the focus on faith and love, for faith and love Erasmus declared to be the essential message of the scripture [**Extract 1**].

That this was moreover a continuing debate can be seen from the kind of questions posed, and the answers given, by a committee of divines which met to consider abuses of the Mass on the very eve of liturgical change in 1547 [**Extract 2**]. Cranmer had evidently moved away from acceptance of transubstantiation some time before the death of Henry and, with such Aristotelian physics behind him, when the second Tudor died the liturgical prowess the archbishop had already shown in the English Litany of 1544 could be indulged to the full. Yet even in 1548 Cranmer was cautious; his *Order of Holy Communion* merely afforded the Mass an English inset of confession, absolution, some 'comfortable words' from scripture, a prayer of 'humble access' and communion in both kinds (wafer-bread and wine). No wonder Brightman regarded it as 'an English supplement to the Latin missal'.

On the symbolic occasion of Whitsunday 1549, the *Book of Common Prayer* came into use. Arguably Cranmer's most enduring achievement, the book and its 1552 revision reduced to the manageable compass of a single volume a whole range of liturgical forms for which medieval clergy had been obliged to refer to five tomes of varying shape, size and weight. The *Missal* contained the ordinary and Canon of the Mass, and the *Breviary* was the book of divine offices, with Kalendar, Psalter and other often varied contents. Then, too, there was the priest's *Manual* (often termed the *Sacerdotal*) and the bishop's *pontifical*; these books set forth sacraments other than the Mass for which priests and bishops were responsible. Finally, there was the often massive *Processional* supplying musical settings for the high and holy days of a colourful period. Although the Sarum Use had become dominant in early sixteenth-century England, it is important to recall that four other Uses - York, Hereford, Bangor and Lincoln - considerably added to the confusion.

When Thomas Cranmer derived a single *Book of Common Prayer* from such complexity, it was thus, by any standards, a remarkable achievement. Moreover, once it is appreciated that his liturgy was not merely an English, or national, rite of the reformation era, but a book of prayer and worship deeply rooted in the Catholic tradition of the Western Church, that achievement is the more remarkable. Simple illustration of Cranmer's skill as a liturgical reformer can mislead if only because of the scale of the undertaking. For F. E. Brightman such study proved a life's work; and although G. J. Cuming's love of liturgy led him to popularise pundits like Brightman and produce a useful textbook for Anglican ordinands, his labours often fail to appreciate the historical significance of Cranmer's immense and timely undertaking. It follows that a focus on primary sources, such as the present volume, can only deal in general principles and set the spotlight on passages to encourage readers to study further themselves. For reasons of space, this is done in two ways.

First, an illustrative chart sets out the sources of Cranmer's inspiration. From early days humanist inquiry had busied his mind not only with the traditional liturgy, received rites and uses of the Western tradition, but also with experimental works such as the *Breviarum Romanum* of the cardinal-general of the Franciscans, Francesco Quiñones, the *Kirchenordnung* of the reforming archbishop of Köln, Hermann von Wied (itself based on collaboration with Martin Bucer) and, of course, the sustained achievement of Martin Luther's essentially conservative re-ordering of worship for Ernestine Saxony.

Secondly, reference to the way Cranmer re-shaped the Eucharist and re-worked the daily offices can conveniently focus in brief compass the principles he observed in fashioning English services for English people. In approaching the Mass, for example, he was clear that notions of propitiatory sacrifice had to be removed, however much an Erasmian urbanity characterised work that approvingly kept

The Great Tradition : A Chart to illustrate the Sources of Thomas Cranmer's inspiration in compiling *The Books of Common Prayer*

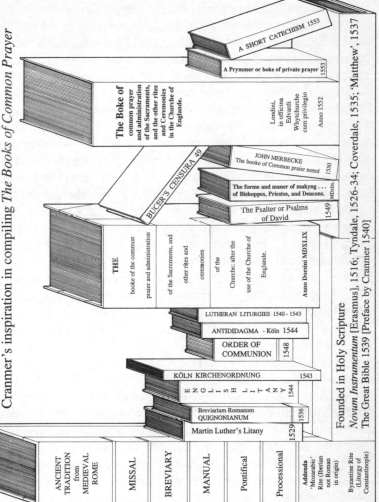

A SHORT CATECHISM 1553

A Prymmer or boke of private prayer — 1553

The Boke of common prayer and administration of the Sacraments, and the other rites and Ceremonies in the Churche of Englande.

Londini, in officina Edvardi Whytchurche cum privilegio — Anno 1552

BUCER'S CENSURA 49

JOHN MERBECKE
The booke of Common praier noted — 1550

The forme and maner of makyng . . . of Bishoppes, Priestes, and Deacons. — MDxlix.

The Psalter or Psalms of David — 1549

THE booke of the common praier and administration of the Sacraments, and other rites and ceremonies of the Churche: after the use of the Churche of Englande.

Anno Domini MDXLIX

LUTHERAN LITURGIES 1540 - 1543

ANTIDIDAGMA - Köln 1544

ORDER OF COMMUNION — 1548

KÖLN KIRCHENORDNUNG — 1543

ENGLISH LITANY — 1544

Breviarium Romanum QUIGNONIANUM — 1536

Martin Luther's Litany — 1529

ANCIENT TRADITION from MEDIEVAL ROME

MISSAL

BREVIARY

MANUAL

Pontifical

Processional

Addenda 'Mozarabic' Rite (Iberian not Roman in origin)

Byzantine Rite (Liturgy of Constantinople)

Founded in Holy Scripture
Novum Instrumentum [Erasmus], 1516; Tyndale, 1526-34; Coverdale, 1535; 'Matthew', 1537
The Great Bible 1539 [Preface by Cranmer 1540]

most of the traditional liturgy. At the outset Cranmer, like Luther before him, continued to celebrate Mass. But while awaiting what the Wittenberger termed 'the coming of the gospel', the archbishop took from the priests those words that treated of sacrifice to provide an altogether different emphasis. To the Canon Cranmer paid most dutiful attention, a true pastor's caution preventing his dropping, as had leading reformers on the continent, what congregations had long been taught to regard as the sacred climax of the liturgy. The celebrant was not to offer the sacrifice *sotto voce*. Cranmer's direction was that the priest, albeit 'turning him to the Altar', was permitted no undertone but was to 'say or sing, plainly and distinctly, this prayer following'. The revised Canon of 'The Supper of the Lord and Holy Communion, commonly called the Mass', transposes the language of sacrifice to dwell on Christ's sacrifice, on the 'sacrifice of praise and thanksgiving', and on the offering by those present of their 'souls and bodies, to be a reasonable, holy, and lively sacrifice'. Nevertheless, the traditional structure of the old Latin service remained: Cranmer's Mass retaining the essential veil of mystery and yet conveying in language of great beauty what was for him the vital heartbeat of Christian proclamation. He himself was evidently well pleased with his new Prayer Book, a liturgy that 'sette forth a very godly ordre agreable to the woorde of God and the primitive Church, verye comfortable to all good people'. But Bishop Gardiner's qualified approbation, and Bishop Hooper's downright disapproval, virtually guaranteed further revision when opportunity allowed.

The fall of Somerset and the Council's quickening Protestant pace under Warwick brought a second Uniformity Bill to the statute book in 1552, and provided a new liturgy that removed all ambiguity from a Eucharist now termed 'The Lord's Supper or Holy Communion'. Unlike its predecessor of 1549, the new Service no longer rehearsed the *Gloria*, but rather the Decalogue, as a prelude to the reading of scripture in set passages for the Epistle and the Gospel of the day. After the Creed and Sermon (the rubric directing a sermon at this point is the only such rubric in the *Book of Common Prayer*, and significant for the reforming insistence that Word and Sacrament go together), the Prayer for the Church, Confession and Absolution all precede that ancient introit to the Canon, the *Sursum corda*. The so-called Prayer of Humble Access, 'We do not presume . . . ' is next [**Extract 3**]. Its new position, and that of the Prayer for the Church, clearly opposes any notion of propitiatory sacrifice or adoration of bread and wine [**Extract 4**]. For the so-called 'consecration' prayer comes next, reciting the scriptural record of Christ's institution. The rubric then requires that 'the minister first receive the Communion in both kinds himself, and next deliver it to other ministers, if any be there present (that they may help the chief minister), and after to the people in their hands kneeling.' After the Communion, all recite the Lord's Prayer aloud. Following at this point, the Prayer of Oblation, now made an alternative to a prayer of thanksgiving, is itself clearly the occasion of congregational self-offering and what was for Cranmer spiritual oblation to God. Coming at this stage too, the *Gloria* is memorably placed to provide Cranmer with a liturgical climax of real insight.

By re-distributing the various components of the old Canon, Cranmer's committee had skilfully played out the sacrifical emphasis that lay at the heart of the medieval Mass, even to the total avoidance of the very word 'consecration'. There is a most striking reference to the new service in an entry in the *Greyfriars' Chronicle* [**Extract 5**].

Having thus most effectively turned the Mass into a Communion, Cranmer turned his attention to the medieval choir office, shortening and simplifying the services in the *Breviary* to provide congregational appeal [**Extract 6**]. Francisco, Cardinal Quiñones admittedly opened the door in this respect, but only Cranmer's grasp and vision could have combined Mattins, Lauds and Prime as 'The Order for Morning Prayer', and Vespers and Compline, arguably the most successful order of them all, as 'The Order for Evening Prayer' (1552). The introit, with its penitential emphasis, introduces much material unknown to the *Breviary*, and recalls for the worshipper scriptural thoughts of penitence and assurance [**Extract 7**]. It is thought to be highly unlikely that Cranmer consciously copied or 'translated' any single source, and rather concluded that he drew on a wide range of liturgical experiment from Quiñones to Hermann, Bucer and Vermiglius. The result is remarkable, being firmly founded in scripture. Paraded in perfection and in sequence are the Psalms, the Old Testament Lesson, first Canticle, New Testament Lesson, and second Canticle - to give a uniquely evangelical perspective to what Luther termed *Gottesdienst*.

That Cranmer was truly a man of common prayer can likewise be seen from his translation and composition of Collects. Precisely defined, a Collect is a short prayer peculiar to the worship of the West that precedes the reading of the Epistle in the Eucharist. Such prayers invoke God, make a specific petition and conclude with an ascription of honour to the Christ whose merits can obtain an answer to the request of his people. Originally derived from the *Sacramentaries* of Leo, Gelasius and Gregory, many Collects had been used in worship since the fifth and sixth centuries. Such hallowed use Cranmer evidently so revered that he either directly translated the Collects into English or, where crude medieval Latin cramped his style (or Church tradition - particularly superstitions surrounding the saints - conflicted with scripture), skilfully paraphrased and augmented the originals. The archbishop clearly never felt himself to be at all restricted by the formal content or phrasing of such sources, so that the soulful creative urges which so characterise his enduring composition are never suffocated. Some Collects he wrote himself, penning remarkable pieces of devotion with a literary merit unparalleled in a vernacular language. Most newly-written Collects related to either significant moments in the Kalendar - crucial teaching seasons in the Church's year like Advent, Christmas and Lent, for example [**Extract 8**] - or to saints' days for which the Latin Collects were unsympathetic to a humanist or reformed commitment [**Extract 9**]. It will be recalled that Erasmus had much to criticise in the *Colloquies* and other satirical sketches about superstitions surrounding the role of lesser saints in Rome's celestial hierarchy.

Much that Cranmer sought to achieve is openly set out in the Preface to the *Book of Common Prayer* [**Extract 10**]; and appendices also explain the attitudes which the archbishop and his committee had to the place of ceremonial in worship [**Extract 11**]. Similarly, much can be gleaned from a glance at various rubrics. For the rest, reaction, both positive and negative in tone, to the changes the liturgy laid down was variously recorded, and for historians of the Church these will naturally remain of abiding interest [**Extract 12**].

Extract 1

Read the New Testament through, you will not find in it any precept which pertains to ceremonies. Where is there a single word of meats or vestments? Where is there any mention of fast...? Love alone He calls His precept. Ceremonies give rise to differences; from love flows peace... And yet we burden those who have been made free by the blood of Christ with all these almost senseless and more than Jewish constitutions.

Erasmus, *Novum instrumentum*.

Extract 2

Quest. 1.

Whether the sacrament of the altar was instituted to be received of one man for another, or to be received of every man for himself?

The sacrament of the altar was not instituted to be received of one man for another, but to be received by every man for himself.

Quest. 2.

Whether the receiving of the said sacrament of one man doth avail and profit any other?

The receiving of the said sacrament by one man doth avail and profit only him that receiveth the same.

Quest. 3.

What is the oblation and sacrifice of Christ in the mass?

The oblation and sacrifice of Christ in the mass is not so called, because Christ indeed is there offered and sacrificed by the priest and the people (for that was done but once by himself upon the cross;) but it is so called, because it is a memory and representation of that very true sacrifice and immolation which before was made upon the cross . . .

Quest. 5.

What time the accustomed order began first in the church, that the priest alone should receive the sacrament?

I think the use, that the priest alone did receive the sacrament without the people, began not within six or seven hundred years after Christ . . .

Quest. 8.

Whether the gospel ought to be taught at the time of the mass, to the understanding of the people being present?

I think it very convenient, that the gospel, concerning the death of Christ and our redemption, should be taught to the people in the mass.

'Questions . . . Concerning some Abuses of the Mass', *Cranmer II*, pp. 150-1.

Extract 3

We do not presume to come to this thy table (O merciful Lord) trusting in our own righteousness, but in thy manifold and great mercies: we be not worthy so much as to gather up the crumbs under thy table: but thou art the same Lord whose property is always to have mercy: Grant us therefore (gracious Lord) so to eat the flesh of thy dear Son Jesus Christ, and to drink his blood* in these holy Mysteries, that we may continually dwell in him, and he in us, that our sinful bodies may be made clean by his body, and our souls washed through his most precious blood. Amen.

* Note the change in wording in The Order of 1552 at this point: 'drink his blood, that our sinful bodies may be made clean by his body, and our souls washed through his most precious blood, and that we may evermore dwell in him, and he in us'.

Liturgies of Edward VI, p. 92; cf., Ibid, pp. 278-9.

Extract 4

Compare 1549:   with 1552:

... Hear us (O merciful Father) we beseech thee; and with thy Holy Spirit and word vouchsafe to bl✠ess and sanc✠tify these thy gifts, and creatures of bread and wine, that they may be unto us the body and blood of thy most dearly beloved son Jesus Christ.

... Hear us, O merciful Father, we beseech thee: and grant that we receiving these thy creatures of bread and wine, according to thy Son our Saviour Jesu Christ's holy institution, in remembrance of his death and passion, may be partakers of his most blessed body and blood: ...

Liturgies of Edward VI, p.88, cf., p.279.

Extract 5

November 1st, 1552

Item, on Allhallow day beganne the boke of the new servis of bred and wyne in Powlles.

Greyfriars Chronicle, edited by J.G. Nichols for the Camden Society (London, 1852), p. 76.

Extract 6

... here is drawn out a Kalendar for that purpose, which is plain and easy to be understood; wherein (so much as may be) the reading of holy scripture is so set forth, that all things shall be done in order, without breaking one piece thereof from another. For this cause be cut off Anthems, Responds, Invitatories [in the Latin rite, Psalm 95 is a good example of such an invitation to prayer] and such like things, as did break the continual course of the reading of the scripture. Yet because there is no remedy, but that of necessity there must be some rules: therefore certain rules are here set forth, which as they be few in number, so they be plain and easy to be understanded. So that here

you have an order for prayer (as touching the reading of holy scripture) much agreeable to the mind and purpose of the old fathers, and a great deal more profitable and commodious, than that which of late was used. It is more profitable, because here are left out many things, whereof some be untrue, some uncertain, some vain and superstitious: and is ordained nothing to be read, but the very pure word of God, the holy scriptures, or that which is evidently grounded upon the same; and that in such a language and order, as is most easy and plain for the understanding, both of the readers and hearers. It is also more commodious, both for the shortness thereof, and for the plainness of the order, and for that the rules be few and easy. Furthermore, by this order, the curates shall need none other books for their public service, but this book and the Bible: by the means whereof, the people shall not be at so great charge for books, as in time past they have been.
Preface to *The Book of Common Prayer*, 1549, in *Liturgies of Edward VI*, pp.18-19.

Extract 7

Dearly beloved brethren, the scripture moveth us in sundry places, to acknowledge and confess our manifold sins and wickedness, and that we should not dissemble nor cloke them before the face of Almighty God our heavenly Father, but confess them with an humble, lowly, penitent and obedient heart: to the end that we may obtain forgiveness of the same by his infinite goodness and mercy. And although we ought at all times humbly to knowledge our sins before God: yet ought we most chiefly so to do, when we assemble and meet together, to render thanks for the great benefits that we have received at his hands, to set forth his most worthy praise, to hear his most holy word, and to ask those things which be requisite and necessary, as well for the body as the soul. Wherefore I pray and beseech you, as many as be here present, to accompany me with a pure heart and humble voice, unto the throne of the heavenly grace, saying after me.

¶ A general confession, to be said of the whole congregation . . . kneeling ALMIGHTY and most merciful Father, we have erred and strayed from thy ways, like lost sheep. We have followed too much the devices and desires of our own hearts. We have offended against thy holy laws. We have left undone those things which we ought to have done, and we have done those things which we ought not to have done, and there is no health in us: but thou, O Lord, have mercy upon us miserable offenders. Spare thou them, O God, which confess their faults. Restore

thou them that be penitent, according to thy promises declared unto mankind, in Christ Jesu our Lord. And grant, O most merciful Father, for his sake, that we may hereafter live a godly, righteous, and sober life, to the glory of thy holy name. Amen.
Liturgies of Edward VI, pp. 218-19.

Extract 8

¶ *The... Collects... to be used at the celebration of the Lord's Supper and Holy Communion, through the year...*

The first Sunday in Advent.

ALMIGHTY God, give us grace that we may cast away the works of darkness, and put upon us the armour of light, now in the time of this mortal life (in the which thy Son Jesus Christ came to visit us in great humility:) that in the last day, when he shall come again in his glorious majesty, to judge both the quick and the dead, we may rise to the life immortal, through him, who liveth and reigneth with thee and the Holy Ghost, now and ever. Amen.

The second Sunday.

BLESSED Lord, which has caused all holy scriptures to be written for our learning: grant us that we may in such wise hear them, read, mark, learn, and inwardly digest them, that by patience and comfort of thy holy word, we may embrace and ever hold fast the blessed hope of everlasting life, which thou hast given us in our Saviour Jesus Christ...

... on Christmas day...

At the second Communion.

ALMIGHTY God, which hast given us thy only-begotten Son to take our nature upon him, and this day to be born of a pure virgin; Grant that we being regenerate, and made thy children by adoption and grace, may daily be renewed by thy holy Spirit, through the same our Lord Jesus Christ, who liveth and reigneth &.

The first day of Lent, commonly called Ashwednesday.

ALMIGHTY and everlasting God, which hatest nothing that thou hast made, and dost forgive the sins of all them that be penitent: Create and make in us new and contrite hearts, that we worthily lamenting our sins, and knowledging our wretchedness, may obtain of thee, the God of all mercy, perfect remission and forgiveness, through Jesus Christ.

The first Sunday in Lent.

O LORD, which for our sake didst fast forty days and forty

nights: Give us grace to use such abstinence, that, our flesh being subdued to the Spirit, we may ever obey thy godly motions [monitions], in righteousness and true holiness, to thy honour and glory, which livest and reignest, &.
Liturgies of Edward VI, pp. 41-3, and p. 49.

Extract 9

Saint Mathie's Day.
The Collect.
ALMIGHTY God, which in the place of the traitor Judas, didst choose thy faithful servant Mathie to be of the number of thy twelve Apostles: Grant that thy church being alway preserved from false Apostles, may be ordered and guided by faithful and true pastors: Through Jesus Christ our Lord. . .
Saint Mark's Day.
The Collect.
ALMIGHTY God, which hast instructed thy holy Church, with the heavenly doctrine of thy Evangelist Saint Mark: give us grace so to be established by thy holy gospel, that we be not, like children, carried away with every blast of vain doctrine: Through Jesus Christ our Lord. . .
Saint Peter's Day.
The Collect.
ALMIGHTY God, which by thy Son Jesus Christ hast given to thy Apostle Saint Peter many excellent gifts, and commandest him earnestly to feed thy flock; make, we beseech thee, all bishops and pastors diligently to preach thy holy word, and the people obediently to follow the same, that they may receive the crown of everlasting Glory, through Jesus Christ our Lord. . .
All Saints.
The Collect.
ALMIGHTY God, which hast knit together thy elect in one communion and fellowship in the mystical body of thy Son Christ our Lord, grant us grace so to follow thy holy Saints in all virtues, and godly living, that we may come to those inspeakable joys, which thou hast prepared for them that unfeignedly love thee; through Jesus Christ.
Liturgies of Edward VI, pp. 69, 70, 72, and 75.

Extract 10

THE PREFACE.

THERE was never any thing by the wit of man so well devised, or so surely established, which (in continuance of time) hath not been corrupted: as ... it may plainly appear by the common prayers in the Church, commonly called divine service: the first original and ground whereof if a man would search out by the ancient fathers, he shall find that the same was not ordained, but of a good purpose, and for a great advancement of godliness: ... that the Clergy, and specially such as were Ministers of the congregation, should (by often reading and meditation of God's word) be stirred up to godliness themselves, and be more able also to exhort other by wholesome doctrine, and to confute them that were adversaries to the truth. And further, that the people (by daily hearing of holy scripture read in the Church) should continually profit more and more in the knowledge of God, and be the more inflamed with the love of his true religion. But these many years passed, this godly and decent order of the ancient fathers hath been so altered, broken, and neglected ... And moreover, whereas St Paul would have such language spoken to the people in the church, as they might understand and have profit by hearing the same; the service in this Church of England (these many years) hath been read in Latin to the people, which they understood not; so that they have heard with their ears only; and their hearts, spirit, and mind, have not been edified thereby ...

Liturgies of Edward VI, pp. 17-18. See also Extract 6 above.

Extract 11

OF CEREMONIES,
WHY SOME BE ABOLISHED AND SOME RETAINED.

Of such ceremonies as be used in the Church, and have had their beginning by the institution of man: Some at the first were of godly intent and purpose devised, and yet at length turned to vanity and superstition: Some entered into the Church by undiscreet devotion, and such a zeal as was without knowledge; and for because they were winked at in the beginning, they grew daily to more and more abuses, which not only for their unprofitableness, but also because they have much blinded the people, and obscured the glory of God, are worthy to be cut away, and clean rejected. Other there be, which although they have been devised by man, yet it is thought good to reserve them still, as well for a decent order in the Church (for the which they were first devised), as because they pertain to edification, whereunto all things done in the Church (as the Apostle teacheth) ought to be referred. And although the keeping or omitting of a ceremony (in itself considered) is but a small thing: yet the wilful and contemptuous transgression, and breaking of a common order, and discipline, is no small offence before God. Let all things be done among you (saith Saint Paul) in a seemly and due order. The appointment of which order pertaineth not to private men: Therefore no man ought to take in hand, nor presume to appoint or alter any public or common order in Christ's Church, except he be lawfully called and authorized thereunto. And whereas, in this our time, the minds of men be so diverse, that some think it a great matter of conscience to depart from a piece of the least of their ceremonies (they be so addicted to their old customs), and again on the other side, some be so new fangle that they would innovate all thing, and so do despise the old that nothing can like them, but that is new: It was thought expedient not so much to have respect how to please and satisfy either of these parties, as how to please God, and profit them both. And yet lest any man should be offended (whom good reason might satisfy), here be certain causes rendered why some of the accustomed ceremonies be put away, and some be retained and kept still.

Some are put away, because the great excess and multitude of them so increased in these latter days, that the burden of them was intolerable*: whereof St Augustine in his time complained, that they were grown to such a number, that the state of Christian people was in worse case (concerning that matter) than were the Jews. And he counselled that such yoke and burden should be taken away, as time would serve quietly to do it. But what would St Augustine have said, if he had seen the ceremonies of late days used among us, whereunto the multitude used in his time was not to be compared? This our excessive multitude of ceremonies was so great, and many of them so dark, that they did more confound and darken, than declare and set forth Christ's benefits unto us. And besides this, Christ's Gospel is not a ceremonial law (as much of Moses' law was); but it is a religion to serve God, not in bondage of the figure or shadow, but in the freedom of spirit, being content only with those ceremonies which do serve to a decent order and godly discipline, and such as be apt to stir up the dull mind of man, to the remembrance of his duty to God, by some notable and special signification, whereby he might be edified.

* The inclusion of this phrase from the general confession of the people before the Eucharist is not merely of interest in itself, but confirms on internal grounds Cranmer's controlling role in the compilation of the Prayer Book appendix OF CEREMONIES. Other clues are, of course, the patristic and Pauline references. *Liturgies of Edward VI*, pp. 155-6.

Extract 12

A letter written by Dryander from Cambridge on 25 March 1549 affords the reader a fresh account of mounting interest and speculation of the kind this Spanish exile was certain would interest his Zurich mentor, Bullinger:

I hear also that a praiseworthy reformation has taken place in matters of religion: it has not yet seen the light, but its promulgation is daily expected. It is generally reported that the mass is abolished, and liberty of marriage allowed to the clergy: which two I consider to be the principal heads of the entire reformation.

Dryander wrote again in June, indicating that the *Book of Common Prayer* had been received by 'the English churches . . . with the greatest satisfaction'. In his earlier letter, he had forthrightly set out his idea of reformation:

the object of which ... is not to form an entire body of christian doctrine, and to deliver a fixed and positive opinion without any ambiguity upon each article, but is entirely directed to the right institution of public worship in churches.

But in this second letter, he returns to the subject of ambiguity, relating it to Cranmer's Communion Service:

... in the cause of religion, which is the most important of all in the whole world, I think that every kind of deception either by ambiguity or trickery of language is altogether unwarrantable. You will also find something to blame in the matter of the Lord's supper; for the book speaks very obscurely, and however you may try to explain it with candour, you cannot avoid great absurdity. The reason is, that the bishops could not of a long time agree among themselves respecting this article, and it was a long and earnest dispute among them whether transubstantiation should be established or rejected. You perceive therefore by this certain proof, that there are no true and solid principles of doctrine in these men, who take a great deal of pains about the most minute and even absurd matters, and neglect those points on

which they ought chiefly to have bestowed their attention. But this is the fate of the church, that the majority overpower the better part; and though many things may be improved, there are nevertheless some causes of offence still remaining.
Original Letters, Vol. I, pp. 349-51.

It was, of course, ambiguity that Gardiner brilliantly used in his passage of arms with Cranmer over the interpretation of crucial prayers in the Canon (1549), namely that the Eucharist 'is by the book of common prayer, being the most true catholic doctrine of the substance of the sacrament, in that it is there so catholicly spoken of', only to receive a categorical refutation in the archbishop's *Answer*.

And as concerning the form of doctrine used in this church of England in the holy communion, that the body and blood of Christ be under the forms of bread and wine, when you shall shew the place where this form of words is expressed, then you shall purge yourself of that, which in the meantime I take to be a plain untruth.
Cranmer I, p. 55; *see also* p. 53.

Shadow-boxing of this kind makes the historian's interpretative task especially difficult, for by itself, liturgy based as it must be on charitable supposition, is intractable as evidence of doctrinal commitment.

With John Hooper, Cranmer's other opponent, fine shades of meaning related to compromise, and such deception was not to be tolerated. In his letter to Bullinger from London on 27 March, Hooper's opposition to the *Book of Common Prayer* was forthright. In time he was to prove so formidable that Cranmer was obliged to reform reformation itself in the revision of 1552:

I can scarcely express to you, my very dear friend, under what difficulties and dangers we are labouring and struggling, that the idol of the mass be thrown out. It is no small hindrance to our exertions, that the form which our senate or parliament, as we commonly call it, has prescribed for the whole realm, is so very defective and of doubtful construction, and in some respects indeed manifestly impious.... I am so much offended with that book, and that not without abundant reason, that if it be not corrected, I neither can nor will communicate with the church in the administration of the supper. *Original Letters*, Vol. I, p. 79.

The premature death of Edward VI brought a Roman Catholic

sovereign to the Tudor throne, and on repealing the Act of Uniformity, Mary and her Council were able to bring back the Mass and a qualified papal supremacy. But this was not to last, and when Elizabeth I brought back a slightly modified *Book of Common Prayer* in 1559, the great Anglican apologist, John Jewel, published the following proud and unrepentant judgement of 'the new religion':

> We truly for our parts ... have done nothing in altering religion, either upon rashness or arrogancy; nor nothing with but good leisure and great consideration. Neither had we ever intended to do it, except both the manifest and most assured will of God, opened to us in his holy scriptures, and the regard of our salvation, had even constrained us thereunto. For, though we have departed from that church, which these men call catholic, and by that means get us envy amongst them that want skill to judge, yet is this enough for us, and it ought to be enough for every wise and good man ... that we have gone from that church which had power to err; which Christ, who cannot err, told so long before it should err; and which we ourselves did evidently see with our eyes to have gone both from the holy fathers, and from the apostles, and from Christ his own self, and from the primitive and catholic church; and we are come, as near as we possibly could, to the church of the apostles and of the old catholic bishops and fathers; which church we know hath hitherto been sound and perfite, and, as Tertullian termeth it, a pure virgin, spotted as yet with no idolatry, nor with any foul or shameful fault; and have directed according to their customs and ordinances not only our doctrine, but also the sacraments, and the form of common prayer.
>
> John Jewel, *An Apology of the Church of England*, Part VI, edited for the Parker Society by J. Ayre in four volumes (Cambridge, 1845-50), Vol. III, p. 100.

6
Defence and Controversy

In order to defend their often dramatic repudiation of medieval Christian tradition, its theory and practice, none of the reformers could avoid controversy. Cranmer was widely respected for his eirenicism, but it was a quality his enemies could confuse with ambiguity. The primate's moderation certainly set him poles apart from men like Bishop Hooper and John Knox. Nevertheless, he was no exception to the general rule, and when pastoral priorities demanded commitment, the archbishop could prove a most formidable opponent. His approach is best seen in a determined defence of the Eucharist. When the *Book of Common Prayer* appeared on Whitsunday 1549, and Cranmer effectively turned the Mass into a Communion, Stephen Gardiner damned the work with faint praise [**Extract 1**]. In his turn, John Hooper deplored the new rite for its timidity [**Extract 2**]. By contrast, Martin Bucer, Strasbourg exile and first-generation reformer, albeit censuring details that did not measure up to his long experience of the best continental churches, saw 'nothing in it ... which is not derived from holy scripture'(*Censura,* p. 44). That Bucer was, however, something of an ecumenical chatterbox can be readily appreciated from a letter he sent from Cambridge to the Lutheran, Brenz [**Extract 3**].

Well aware that precipitate action could endanger the cause, Cranmer proceeded with cautious deference. Forthright in sermons [**Extract 4**] and homilies [**Extract 5**], his debating style when the House of Lords discussed the sacrament (14-18 December, 1548) was one of quiet insistence and dependence on his grasp of patristic interpretation [**Extract 6**]. The threat posed by the Devon rebels may have paralleled the problem Luther had faced during the German Peasants' Revolt twenty-five years earlier (1525), but Cranmer's stern approach effectively saved the day [**Extract 7**].

Cranmer wrote the *Defence of the True and Catholic Doctrine of the Supper of the Lord* to justify his understanding of the Eucharist from scripture and the early Fathers [**Extract 8**]. It was a tract that also emphasised the sacramental doctrine enshrined in the *Book of Common Prayer* published the previous year. If Stephen Gardiner, Bishop of Winchester, had chosen to praise that for being 'not distant from the catholic faith' [see **Extract 1**], his *Confutation* (1551) of the *Defence* infuriated Cranmer by charging the primate with inconsistency. In his *Answer* to what he termed Gardiner's 'crafty and sophistical cavillation' (published that same year), Cranmer revealed himself as a master of the keys in controversy, a truly dramatic use of the diapason stop enabling him to blast his adversary and rival in a *cause célèbre* he undoubtedly made his own [**Extract 9**].

Extract 1

Gardiner was later to stir up a great deal of trouble for Cranmer over this matter. Prior to his trial at Lambeth in January 1551, the bishop of Winchester had made use of a sojourn in the Tower of London to write against his archbishop. In particular, he maintained that the mystery of the Eucharist set out in the *Book of Common Prayer* (1549) was 'not distant from the catholic faith, in my judgement'. Gardiner scored debating points with skilful polemic that drew attention to ambiguities which, he said, made it difficult for him to believe that Cranmer could really reconcile 1549 Prayer-Book teaching with the argument of the archbishop's *Defence* of 1550. Briefly, Gardiner held that the words used in the administration of the elements - 'body' and 'bloud' - implied the traditional understanding (transubstantiation), and that the consecration prayer had to be interpreted in the same way. He also held that the use of a prayer for the departed in such a context must mean that the Mass was intended as a propitiatory sacrifice for the sins of the living and the dead, and that the inclusion of a prayer of humble access could only mean that adoration of Christ in the sacrament was intended.

Cranmer's annoyance peppered his *Answer* to Gardiner, a work indicating on every page that the primate's patience was exhausted, and clearly showing how much he resented the charge of ambiguity: 'Although my chief study be to speak so plainly that all men may understand everything what I say, yet nothing is plain to him that will find knots in a rush.'

Cranmer I, p. 140; the edition also prints Gardiner's tract in full.

THE PRINCIPAL LITURGIES OF EARLY PROTESTANTISM

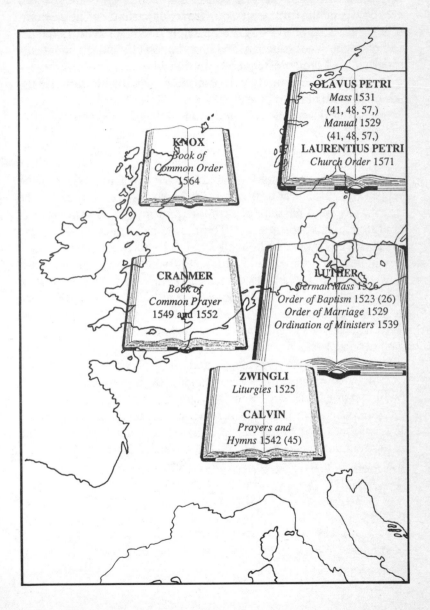

OLAVUS PETRI
Mass 1531
(41, 48, 57,)
Manual 1529
(41, 48, 57,)
LAURENTIUS PETRI
Church Order 1571

KNOX
*Book of
Common Order*
1564

CRANMER
*Book of
Common Prayer*
1549 and 1552

LUTHER
German Mass 1526
Order of Baptism 1523 (26)
Order of Marriage 1529
Ordination of Ministers 1539

ZWINGLI
Liturgies 1525

CALVIN
*Prayers and
Hymns* 1542 (45)

Extract 2

I can scarcely express to you, my very dear friend, under what difficulties and dangers we are labouring and struggling, that the idol of the mass may be thrown out. It is no small hindrance to our exertions, that the form which our senate or parliament, as we commonly call it, has prescribed for the whole realm, is so very defective and of doubtful construction, and in some respects indeed manifestly impious . . . I am so offended with that book . . . that if it be not corrected, I neither can nor will communicate with the church in the administration of the supper.

John Hooper to Henry Bullinger, from London, 27 March 1550; *Original Letters*, Vol. I, p. 79.

Extract 3

No one has as yet found fault with me for my simple view of the subject; nor have I ever heard of any one who has been able to confute it from any solid passage of scripture, nor indeed has any one yet ventured to make the attempt. Their principal argument is, that the mysteries of Christ can be well and intelligibly explained; (which would be true, if they would add, 'to faith, but not to reason'). They now assume, that it cannot with reason be supposed of Christ, that he is in heaven without being circumscribed by physical space; and since he is thus in heaven, as they take for granted, they insist, not only upon what no one will allow them, but also without any solid reason, that it cannot be understood that the same body of Christ is in heaven and in the supper: and when we reply, that no one supposes a local presence of Christ in the supper, they again say that the body of Christ cannot be understood to be present any where without being locally circumscribed. The sum therefore of their argument is to this effect. Reason does not comprehend what you teach respecting the exhibition and presence of Christ in the supper; therefore they are not true, and the scriptures which seem to prove them must be otherwise interpreted. . . I have as yet met with no real Christians who were not entirely satisfied with our simple view . . . as soon as it had been properly explained to them. I wish you and all yours every happiness in the Lord. Cambridge, May 15, 1550.

Martin Bucer to Johannes Brenz; *Original Letters* Vol. II, pp. 544-5.

Extract 4

Writing to counsel Hugh Latimer about preaching at Court, Cranmer
was clear that, 'in any condition you stand no longer in the pulpit than
an hour, or an hour and a half at the most'. He urged biblical emphases
on his correspondent:

> take for your purpose some processes of scripture, the gospel,
> pistill, or any other part of scripture ... to expound and declare
> according to the pure sense and meaning ... be very circumspect
> to overpass and omit all manner speech, either apertly or suspi-
> ciously sounding against any special man's facts, acts, manners,
> or sayings ... which would seem to many that you were void of
> charity ... Nevertheless, if such occasion be given by the word
> of God, let none offence or superstition be unreprehended,
> specially if it be generally spoken, without affection.
> *Cranmer II*, p. 308.

Extract 5

Without faith all that is done of us is but dead before God, although the
work seem never so gay and glorious before man. Even as a picture
graven or painted is but a dead representation of the thing itself, and is
without life, or any manner of moving; so be the works of all unfaithful
persons before God. They do appear to be lively works, and indeed
they be but dead, not availing to the eternal life. They be but shadows
and shews of lively and good things, and not good and lively things
indeed; for true faith doth give life to the works, and out of such faith
come good works, that be very good works indeed; and without it no
work is good before God.
Homily of Good Works Annexed unto Faith, 1547; in *Cranmer II*, p. 141.

Extract 6

The famous debate in the House of Lords, although recorded in MS as
'Certayne Notes touching the Disputacions of the Byshoppes in this
last Parliament assembled', is no equivalent of *Hansard*, and tantalis-
ing by its brevity. On the other hand, it clearly reveals a Cranmer
quietly insistent for 'the new religion' in terms of a sacramental
allegiance held by the Swiss and those influenced by Bucer. The archbishop is thus not merely opposed to the received doctrines of transubstantiation and real presence resulting in adoration of the consecrated
host, but clearly testified that the sacrament: 'was ordeyned to be eaten
of theym ... But they saye the very bodie is there when yt is hanged

upp, which is not founde in Scripture.' Likewise, the primate informed their lordships that: 'Eating with his mouth gyveth nothing to man, nor the bodye being in the bread . . . [for] . . . we cannot eate his bodye indeade'.

Later in the great debate Canterbury's gracious refrain was heard like the still small voice it was in the midst of an otherwise dramatic furore, Cranmer remarking in simple, effective style that: 'To have Christ present really here, when I may receave hym in faith, is not avayleable to do me goode.' His argument was, of course, closely related to his grasp of justification by faith alone: 'They be twoo things to eate the sacrament and to eate the bodie of Christ. The eating of the bodie is to dwell in Christ, and this may be thoo a man never taste the Sacrament.' And, in much the same context: 'He that maketh a will beaquiethes certayne Legaces, and this is our Legacy, Remission of synnes, which those onelie receave that are membres of his body.'

Then, too, central to Cranmer's contribution to the debate, was a scholarly reliance on scripture and the Fathers as the staple of an argument far removed from the rationalism of scholasticism and Aristotelian physics. 'Scripture and doctours prove that *Hic calix* is *figurative* which he often used and *significabat vinum*,' Cranmer argued, making classic appeal to the apostolic letter sent to the young church at Corinth, much-valued evidence used to set out the characteristic case of the party of reform.

Seynte Paul saythe *Panis quem frangimus est communicacio Corporis*. Evyn so Christ when he sayde *This is my bodye* he ment *communionem corporis*. For Christ when he byddes us eate his bodye it is *figurative*; for we cannot eate his bodye indeade.

Reference is also made to Augustine, Cyprian, Cyril, Epiphanius and Irenaeus. The frequent appeal to Tertullian moreover provides a striking parallel with the understanding of the Swiss Reformer, Oecolampadius of Basel, that 'godly and excellent learned man' whose *De genuina verborum Christi* (1525) was not only well-known to Cranmer, but provided a major source for his *Defence*. The MS entitled 'Certayne Notes' is MS Royal 17B XXXIX in the British Library. A transcript can be found as an appendix to J.T. Tomlinson, *The Great Parliamentary Debate in 1548 on the Lord's Supper* (London, n.d.).

Extract 7

. . . my duty unto God, and the pity that I have of your ignorance, move me now at this time to open plainly and particularly your own articles unto you, that you may understand them, and no longer be deceived.

YOUR FIRST ARTICLE IS THUS:
We will have all the general councils, and holy decrees of our forefathers, observed, kept, and performed . . .

First, to begin with the manner of your phrase. Is this the fashion of subjects to speak unto their prince. 'We will have?' . . . If you be subjects, then I admonish you, as St Paul taught Silas, saying, 'Warn them to be subject to princes and rulers, obliging them at a word.'. . . Your servants be by the scripture commanded, as they fear God, to be obedient to their masters, whether their masters be good or evil. . .

THE THIRD ARTICLE
We will have the mass in Latin, as was before, and celebrated by the priest, without any man or woman communicating with him.

Forasmuch as there is nothing with you but *will* let your will be conferred with reason and God's word . . . For all the whole that is done should be the act of the people and pertain to the people, as well as to the priest . . . Will you not understand what the priest prayeth for you, what thanks he giveth for you, what he asketh for you? . . . Had you rather be like pies or parrots, that be taught to speak, and yet understand not one word what they say, than be true christian men, that pray unto God in heart and in faith? The priest is your proctor and attorney, to plead your cause, and to speak for you all; and had you rather not know than know what he saith for you? . . .

YOUR FIFTH ARTICLE IS THIS:
We will have the sacrament of the altar but at Easter delivered to the lay-people; and then but in one kind.

Methinks you be like a man that were brought up in a dark dungeon, that never saw light, nor knew nothing that is abroad in the world. And if a friend of his, pitying his ignorance and state, would bring him out of his dungeon, that he might see the light and come to knowledge, he, being from his youth used to darkness, could not abide the light, and would willingly shut his eyes, and be offended both with the light, and with his friend also. A most godly prince of famous memory, king Henry VIII, our late sovereign lord, pitying to see his subjects many years so brought up in darkness and ignorance of God by the erroneous doctrine and superstitions of the bishop of Rome, with the counsel of all his nobles and learned men, studied by all means, and that to his no little danger and charges, to bring you out of your said ignorance and darkness unto the true light and knowledge of God's word. And our most dread sovereign lord that now is, succeeding his father . . . hath with no less care and diligence studied to perform his father's godly intent and purpose . . . All learned men and godly have exhorted christian people (although they have not commanded them) often to receive the communion. And in the apostles' time the people at Jerusalem received it every day, as it appears by the manifest word of the scripture. And after, they received it in some places every day; in some places four times in the week; in some three times; some twice; commonly everywhere at the least once in the week. . . .

YOUR EIGHTH ARTICLE IS THIS:

We will not receive the new service, because it is but like a Christmas game; but we will have our old service of matins, mass, even-song, and procession in Latin, as it was before. And so we the Cornish men, whereof certain of us understand no English, utterly refuse this new English.

As concerning the having of the service in the Latin tongue, is sufficiently spoken of in the answer to your third article. But I would gladly know the reason why the Cornish men refuse utterly the new English, as you call it, because certain of you understand it not; and yet you will have the service in Latin, which almost none of you understand. If this be a sufficient cause for Cornwall to refuse the English service, because some of you understand none English, a much greater cause have they, both of Cornwall and Devonshire, to refuse utterly the late service; forasmuch as fewer of them know the Latin tongue than they of Cornwall the English tongue. But where you say that you will have the old service, because the new is 'like a Christmas game', you declare yourselves what spirit you be led withal, or rather what spirit leadeth them that persuaded you that the word of God is but like a Christmas game. It is more like a game and a fond play to be laughed at of all men, to hear the priest speak aloud to the people in Latin, and the people listen with their ears to hear; and some walking up and down in the church, some saying other prayers in Latin, and none understandeth other. Neither the priest nor his parish wot what they say. And many times the thing that the priest sayeth in Latin is so fond of itself, that it is more like a play than a godly prayer. . . .

But forasmuch as you understand not the old Latin service, I shall rehearse some things in English that were wont to be read in Latin, that when you understand them, you may judge them whether they seem to be true tales, or fables; and whether they or God's word seem to be more like plays and Christmas games. 'The devil entered into a certain person, in whose mouth St Martin put his finger; and because the devil could not get out at his mouth, the man blew him out behind.' This is one of the tales that was wont to be read in the Latin service, that you will needs have again. As though the devil had a body, and that so crass that he could not pass out by the small pores of the flesh, but must needs have a wide hole to go out at. Is this a grave and godly matter to be read in the church, or rather a foolish Christmas tale, or an old wives' fable, worthy to be laughed at and scorned of every man that hath either wit or godly judgement?

Answers to the Fifteen Articles of the Devon Rebels, 1549; in *Cranmer II*, p.163ff.

Extract 8

Although in this treaty of the sacrament of the body and blood of our Saviour Christ, I have already sufficiently declared the institution and meaning of the same, according to the very words of the Gospel and of St Paul, yet it shall not be in vain somewhat more at large to declare the same, according to the mind as well of holy Scripture as of old ancient authors; and that so sincerely and plainly, without doubts, ambiguities, or vain questions, that the very simple and unlearned people may easily understand the same, and be edified thereby. And this by God's grace is mine only intent and desire, that the flock of Christ dispersed in this realm (among whom I am appointed a special pastor) may no longer lack the commodity and fruit which springeth of this heavenly knowledge. For the more clearly it is understood, the more sweetness, fruit, comfort, and edification it bringeth to the godly receivers thereof.

Defence, edited by C.H.H. Wright (London 1928), p. 11.

Extract 9

Here before the beginning of your book you have prefixed a goodly title; but it agreeth with the argument and matter thereof, as water agreeth with the fire. For your book is so far from an explication and assertion of the true catholic faith in the matter of the sacrament, that it is but a crafty cavillation and subtle sophistication, to obscure the truth thereof, and to hide the same, that it should not appear. And in your whole book, the reader (if he mark it well) shall easily perceive, how little learning is shewed therein, and how few authors you have alleged, other than such as I brought forth in my book, and made answer unto: but there is shewed what may be done by fine wit and new devices to deceive the reader, and by false interpretations to avoid the plain words of scripture and of the old authors. . .

This bladder is so puffed up with wind, that it is marvel it brasteth not. But be patient awhile, good reader, and suffer until the blast of wind be past, and thou shalt see a great calm, the bladder broken, and nothing in it but all vanity. . .

I see well you would take a dung-fork to fight with, rather than you would lack a weapon.

Answer, in Cranmer I, pp. 9, 133, 137.

In a real sense, the engagement between Gardiner and Cranmer engendered more sound, heat and fury than light. Moreover, because the former bishop of Winchester had followed canon law as a postgraduate discipline at Cambridge, where Cranmer had been a devotee of 'the new divinity', little true engagement of minds proved possible. The battle between them is best likened to a bout of shadow-boxing in which exponents of very different disciplines attempt to score off one another. Two further passages from the *Answer,* both of them brief, illustrate the argument:

Here may all men of judgement see by experience, how divinity is handled when it cometh to the discussion of ignorant lawyers.
Cranmer I, p. 157.

In this point I will join a plain issue with you, that I neither willingly go about to deceive the reader in the searching of St Augustine (as you use to do in every place) nor have I not trusted my 'man or friend' herein (as it seemeth you have done overmuch) but I have diligently expended and weighed the matter myself. For although in such weighty matters of scripture and ancient authors you must needs trust your men (without whom I know you can do very little, being brought up from your tender age in other kinds of study) yet I, having exercised myself in the study of scripture and divinity from my youth (whereof I give most hearty lauds and thanks to God) have learned now to go alone, and do examine, judge, and write all such weighty matters myself; Although, I thank God, I am neither so arrogant nor so wilful, that I will refuse the good advice, counsel, and admonition of any man, be he man or master, friend or foe. . . .

And I have not so far overshot myself or been overseen, that I would have attempted to publish this matter, if I had not before-hand excussed the whole truth therein from the bottom. But because I myself am certain of the truth (which hath been hid these many years, and persecuted by the papists with fire and fagot, and should be so yet still if you might have your own will), and because also I am desirous that all my countrymen of England (unto whom I have no small cure and charge to tell the truth) should no longer be kept from the same truth; therefore have I published the truth which I know in the English tongue, to the intent that I may edify all by that tongue, which all do perfectly know and understand. Which my doing, it seemeth, you take in very evil part, and be not a little grieved thereat, because you would rather have the light of truth hid still under the bushel, than openly to be set abroad that all men may see it.

Cranmer I, pp. 223-4. The *Answer* is printed side by side with Gardiner's *Confutation* in the Parker Society volume edited by J.E. Cox (Cambridge, 1844).

7

'Given to Hospitality'

In an age when religion was politics and politics religion, Church reform was often so dependent on statecraft as to have about it a 'stop -go' dimension. But for the support of his own prince, Martin Luther could not have successfully defied the panoply of power ranged against him at the Diet of Worms (1521); and much of the mystery surrounding the ministry of Thomas Cranmer in England relates to the primatial deference of an archbishop who sought to achieve *modus vivendi* with a trying Tudor king. By the ingenious and complex legal procedures of the so-called Reformation Parliament (1529-36), Henry VIII had set up in business as 'Head of the Church'; and, having been raised to his own ecclesiastical eminence by such a 'godly prince', Cranmer could but defer to the 'Lord High Executioner' if his reforming vision was to have any hope of implementation.

Few in number, the early reformers led dangerous and lonely lives. When crises came, the fellowship such men evidently experienced in the 'good old cause' of the gospel was much enlivened both by correspondence and, at times, personal contact and collaboration. For example, when Cranmer was dispirited after the execution of Cromwell and the ascendancy of that shrewd traditionalist and rival of his, Stephen Gardiner, a letter from Martin Bucer certainly worked wonders. Later, when Charles V's Diet accepted the Augsburg *Interim* (June 1548), with devastating implications for Church reform in the imperial city of Strasbourg, Cranmer's invitation to Bucer to come to Lambeth resulted in a rescue operation, that brought one of Europe's leading Protestant theologians to England.

Cranmer came early to respect Bucer's eirenical approach, and the Strasbourg Reformer was clearly embarrassed by the English archbishop's fulsome praise and 'excessive liberality' for Bucer's dedication in his *Commentary on the Epistle to the Romans*, (1536) [**Extract 1**]. In marked contrast to the great Erasmus, who sought the widest possible patronage, it seems that Bucer did not hope for financial return from such dedications. Although he would have had no real grasp of the English situation, moreover, his dramatic life had about it a biblical quality which revealed his missionary intentions. Bucer thus claimed Cranmer for a cause that made them 'brethren and members of the same body'. He felt the Reformation to be under constant threat and, particularly anxious about prospects in the Tudor kingdom, he was clear that doctrinal priority had to be given to 'that chief head of christian doctrine . . . justification' [**Extract 2**].

A shared liturgical interest also kept the Reformers in touch, Cranmer so valuing the counsel Bucer gave Hermann of Köln that he later used it in part himself when revising English church services. Accordingly, when the *Interim* was enforced, and Protestant ministry in Strasbourg was officially proscribed, Cranmer's invitation, as a Macedonian call, proved so timely that Bucer took it to be a vocational summons [**Extract 3**]. As he wrote in solemn style, 'there appears no reason for us to doubt, that we hear from your reverence the voice of Christ'. Temporising in the tents of Kedar was not for him, and by April 1549, with his wife and little daughter together with his colleague and travelling companion Paul Fagius, Martin Bucer had reached Lambeth, and 'from the house of the archbishop of Canterbury, near London', wrote back to inform a remnant of the Strasbourg pastorate that they had been 'received and entertained . . . as brethren, not as dependents'.

For his own part, Cranmer made the most of the presence of both Bucer and Fagius. First they spent the Long Vacation, before either University could claim them, with him at his palace at Croydon. There they began work on a Latin bible, Fagius taking the Old and Bucer the New Testament. But this was not before Cranmer had presented his distinguished scholarly visitors at Court. A letter of Fagius outlines for Conrad Hubert and the Strasbourg fraternity their meeting with Protector Somerset and the 'very young . . . very handsome' king who 'gives for his age such wonderful proofs of piety' [**Extract 4**]. Then, too, although Cranmer had hoped Fagius would go to Oxford to join Vermiglius at 'the most celebrated' University, the archbishop evidently heeded his request not to be separated from Bucer. In consequence, Cambridge reaped the benefit, Bucer and Fagius gaining appointment to Regius Professorships in Divinity and Hebrew respectively from Michaelmas 1549. When Fagius died shortly afterwards (on 13 November), the joint biblical venture had to be abandoned. It was a sad report Bucer sent to Strasbourg, the loss of his colleague prompting him to make observations on the worrying facts that the English 'people are still without pastors' and that his own health was 'in a very doubtful and unsatisfactory state'. Cranmer and the king had done their best to care for his human frailty, their gifts being stoves to provide extra heating in an effort to keep at least some of the Fenland chill from penetrating Bucer's old bones. Without his 'usual wine and diet' and 'utterly unable to bear the cold', the Strasbourg exile became a pathetic figure at the last. But he worked hard regardless. His *Censure* of the *Book of Common Prayer* (1549) and particularly the tract *On the Kingdom of Christ*, which he prepared as a New Year gift to be presented to Edward VI in 1551, constituted a considerable achievement in trying times [**Extract 5**].

Real enough in itself, Cranmer's hospitality also had a wider purpose for the archbishop drew on an idealised vision of apostolic and early Christian precedent. The reformed cause had shown itself sadly divided over crucial issues like the Eucharist; and, now the Council of Trent had been convened, it was the statesman in Cranmer who wrote in diplomatic vein, like a lesser Calvin. Addressed to John Laski, Albert Hardenburg, Philip Melanchthon and, among others, Calvin himself, his correspondence offered England as a venue where 'wise and godly men should take counsel together' (as he suggested to Melanchthon) and, in deliberations designed to achieve unity, embrace 'the chief subjects of ecclesiastical doctrine, and transmit the truth uncorrupted to posterity'. Bullinger had written to seek assurance that no English delegate would be sent to Trent, and Cranmer's prompt rejoinder on that score outlined for the Zürich Reformer plans for 'a godly synod' in England [**Extract 6**]. Evidently much exercised over the Tridentine decree 'respecting the worship of the host' - the Council had passed its eucharistic canon at Session XIII the previous autumn - he wrote to Calvin on the same day, clear in his mind, 'not only that we may guard others against this idolatry, but also . . . ourselves come to an agreement upon the doctrine of this sacrament'. A week later, in a letter to Melanchthon, Cranmer wrote that he wished the reformed Churches would follow apostolic precedent by meeting together to 'declare their judgement as well respecting other subjects of dispute . . . and attest their agreement by some published document'. [**Extract 7**] Nothing came of the project, although Calvin in his reply to Cranmer expressed himself willing 'to cross ten seas' if he could help to heal the bleeding and broken body that was Christ's Church.

THE
GREAT EUCHARISTIC DIVIDE

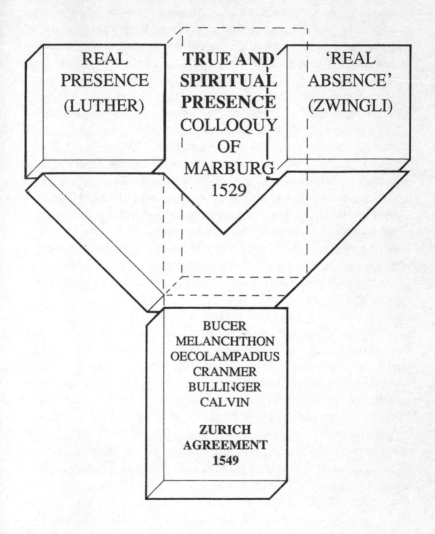

REAL PRESENCE (LUTHER)

TRUE AND SPIRITUAL PRESENCE
COLLOQUY OF MARBURG 1529

'REAL ABSENCE' (ZWINGLI)

BUCER
MELANCHTHON
OECOLAMPADIUS
CRANMER
BULLINGER
CALVIN

ZURICH AGREEMENT 1549

Cranmer did not merely place eminent theologians in the influential groves of academe: he also did much to care for all sorts and conditions of Protestant faithful fleeing before mounting persecution from papal and imperial authorities on the continent. Particularly anxious to afford such *émigrés* a central place of worship of their own, the archbishop was instrumental in securing by letters patent the 'church that was formerly the Augustines', renamed as *Templum Domini Jesu*, to be their shrine; he also arranged for it to be refurbished at royal expense.

> We command and strictly charge the Mayor, Sheriffs and Aldermen of our City of London, the Bishop of London and his successors, with all other Archbishops, Bishops, Justices, and Ministers of ours whatsoever, that they permit the aforesaid, the Superintendent and Ministers and their successors, freely and peacefully to enjoy [gaudere], use and conduct their own rites and ceremonies and their own particular ecclesiastical discipline, notwithstanding that they do not agree with the rites and ceremonies customary in our own kingdom, without impeachment, molestation or disturbance of them, or of any one of them, by any statute, act, proclamation, injunction, restraint or use to the contrary previously made, issued, or promulgated to the contrary . . .
>
> Burnet, Vol. V, pp. 307-8 (Record LI).

Doubtless deeming this to be the thin end of a wedge that could make nonsense of the Act of Uniformity, Bishop Nicholas Ridley argued for a narrow law-and-order theology that evidently displeased such sects. Written to keep Bullinger informed, a fascinating letter of another exile, Martin Micronius, shrewdly assessed the interplay of events and personalities that combined to afford *émigrés* freedom of worship. He recorded the sympathy of 'Master Hooper, most vigilant prelate'; the favour of Edward VI, 'discreet and godly king'; the delaying tactics of the Lord Treasurer, (Sir Thomas Cheyney), 'mouth-piece of the bishops'; the determined opposition of Ridley; and, above all, the support of the 'archbishop of Canterbury, the especial patron of the foreigners' [**Extract 8**].

Ridley's action was shrewd in so far as it was his responsibility as a diocesan bishop to view such extremes of radicalism, almost like Bruegel-Bosch fantasies, with grave suspicion. Overruling his most significant colleague, Cranmer evidently felt it was best to trust Superintendent Laski to deal with any threat of heresy himself. It was a remarkable gesture of magnanimity by which the archbishop effectively welcomed the strangers into his own household.

Extract 1

I am not of so ingenuous a disposition as to be amended by praise, but require rather to be disciplined by plain and severe chastisement. Besides, the commendation I read in your letter is so excessive, as to grieve me exceedingly. I attribute, however, that writing to your troublesome engagements, which are all but killing you, not to say that they sometimes cause you to forget yourself: otherwise I should be very sorry that you did not exercise towards me paternal *severity*, I will not say *verity*. I am well aware of the defects that are to be found in my writings; and unless I thought that some of the more unlearned might perhaps be benefited by them, by accustoming themselves to handle the scriptures with somewhat greater accuracy, I am aware that it would have been intolerable presumption in me to have published a single page, and especially at a period so abounding in learning. I was moreover in circumstances of the greatest disquiet, and obliged to hurry every thing most prodigiously while I was writing my commentary on the Romans: wherefore I am well aware that there are innumerable defects in that work which even the most indulgent partiality must necessarily condemn. You have stated, however, the plan which you desire to lay down for these writings; and in this I acknowledge your paternal admonition, for which also I offer my best thanks. And I wish that I may be able to follow the method which you point out, since I am sensible it will be of the greatest benefit to the churches.

Bucer to Cranmer, from Strasbourg, 29 October 1539; in *Original Letters*, Vol. II, p. 522.

Extract 2

I am writing to you of these things, that you may see that we are anxious about you all; and if we could only discover by what means we might be able to help you, it would be our greatest delight to afford such assistance as is due from brethren and members of the same body. The Lord grant in the mean time, that you may faithfully retain and rightly explain that chief head of christian doctrine, namely, the article of justification. For as long as that is retained in the churches, even in any degree, the kingdom of Christ will yet remain amongst you.

Ibid., p. 530.

Extract 3

I have read your letter ... in which you relate the miserable condition of Germany, and inform us that you can scarcely preside in the ministry of the word in your city. With groanings therefore I call out with the prophet, 'Show thy marvellous loving-kindness, O thou that savest them which trust in thee from those that rise up against thy right hand' [*Margin*, Psalm 17, verse 7]. Nor do I doubt but that God will regard both this and the like lamentations of godly men; and that he will preserve and defend the true doctrine, which has hitherto been sincerely set forth in your churches, against all the rage of the devil and of the world. Those, in the mean time, who are unable amidst the raging storm to launch out into the deep, must take refuge in harbour. To you, therefore, my Bucer, our kingdom will be a most safe harbour, in which, by the blessing of God, the seeds of true doctrine have happily begun to be sown. Come over therefore to us, and become a labourer with us in the harvest of the Lord.

Cranmer to Bucer, from London, 2 October 1548; in *Original Letters*, Vol. I, pp. 19-20.

Extract 4

On the first day of May we removed from Lambeth to Croydon, where the archbishop generally passes the summer. On the fifth of the same month we were taken to Court, where access to the King's majesty was granted us immediately after dinner. I cannot express with what kindness we were received by him, as well as by the Lord Protector, and others of the nobility, and how he congratulated us upon our arrival. This, indeed, exhilarated us beyond measure. Though he is still very young, and very handsome, he gives for his age such wonderful proofs of his piety, as that the whole kingdom and all godly persons entertain the greatest hopes of him. May our good and gracious God preserve him in safety many years, that he may be able to govern the kingdom long and happily, and at the same time to advance in various ways the kingdom of Christ, which we ought all of us to entreat for him from God with fervent prayers.

Fagius to Hubert, from Croydon, 7 May 1549; in *Original Letters*, Vol. I, pp. 333-4.

Extract 5

... what would I not do for Your Majesty, if only I might accomplish or produce something pleasing to him who has so kindly received as exiles into his kingdom both me and Paul Fagius of blessed memory, that very select vessel of Christ our Saviour; in addition to this, he committed to us the sacred trust of explaining Holy Scripture in this illustrious University of his at so very generous a salary, which he even wished us to enjoy during the months when, hindered by ill health, we were able to do nothing at all in the work of our ministry. But Your Majesty's kindness was by no means satisfied with this; he added a splendid gift of twenty pounds with which I might obtain, not so much a convenience as a necessity, a stove to warm my frail body, exhausted as I am by age and broken by sickness. When I am now comfortably warmed by it, I rightly beg the Lord to warm and foster Your Majesty with the fire of his love and the kindling of every blessing, keeping from him everything cold, whether it be a matter of sins or of disasters and sorrows.

De Regno Christi, edited by W. Pauck for the Library of Christian Classics (Philadelphia and London, 1969), Vol. 19, pp. 174-5.

Extract 6

You write to me ... that I would advise the King's majesty not to send any delegate to the council of Trent, there was no need of any advice of mine to dissuade him from a measure which never came into his mind: but I considered it better, forasmuch as our adversaries are now holding their councils at Trent to confirm their errors, to recommend his majesty to grant his assistance, that in England, or elsewhere, there might be convoked a synod of the most learned and excellent persons, in which provision might be made for the purity of ecclesiastical doctrine, and especially for an agreement upon the sacramentarian controversy.

Cranmer to Bullinger, from Lambeth, 20 March 1552; in *Original Letters*, Vol. I. p. 23.

Extract 7

We read in the *Acts of the Apostles*, that when a dispute had arisen, as to whether those who from among the Gentiles had been turned to God, should be compelled to be circumcised, and keep the law of Moses, the apostles and elders came together to consider of this matter; and having compared their opinions, delivered the judgement of their council in a written epistle. This example I wish we ourselves could imitate, in whose churches the doctrine of the gospel has been restored and purified. But although all controversies cannot be removed in this world (because the party which is hostile to the truth, will not assent to the judgement of the church), it is nevertheless to be desired that the members of the true church should agree among themselves upon the chief heads of ecclesiastical doctrine. But it cannot escape your notice, how greatly religious dissensions, especially in the matter of the Lord's Supper, have rent the churches asunder: had they been settled before, the Emperor, I think, would never have made war against you. And it is truly grievous that the sacrament of unity is made by the malice of the devil food for disagreement, and, as it were, the apple of contention. I could wish therefore, that those who excel others in erudition and judgement, should be assembled together, after the example of the apostles, and declare their judgement as well respecting other subjects of dispute, as likewise especially respecting this controversy, and attest their agreement by some published document.

Cranmer to Melanchthon, from Lambeth, 27 March 1552; in *Original Letters*, Vol. I, pp. 25-6.

Extract 8

Blessed be God, who has bestowed upon England a discreet and godly king, who most diligently purifies and gathers together the church of Christ. By his favour the church that was formerly the Augustines' has been made over to the German and French foreigners, that they may have the pure ministry of the word and sacraments, according to the apostolic form. We are altogether exempted, by the letters patent of the king and council, from the jurisdiction of the bishops. To each church (I mean the German and French) are assigned by the king two ministers of the word (among whom is my unworthy self), over whom has been appointed superintendent the most illustrious John à Lasco [Laski the Polish *émigré* viz.]; by whose aid alone, under God, we foreigners have arrived at our present state of pure religion. Some of the bishops, and especially the bishop of London [Ridley], with certain others, are opposed to our design; but I hope their opposition will be ineffectual. The archbishop of Canterbury, the especial patron of the foreigners, has been the chief support and promoter of our church, to the great astonishment of some; but God can make use of all persons to the advancement of his glory.

Micronius to Bullinger, from London, 28 August 1550; in *Original Letters*, Vol. II, pp. 567-8.

8
The Time of Tribulation

Once Northumberland had secured the archbishop's signature on the 'device' designed to alter the succession in favour of what was effectively a Dudley dynasty, Cranmer could expect no quarter from the Marian authorities. Compassion had compelled duty to the dying king, and he could not possibly have withheld outward approval of an end the boy had been convinced would save the 'true religion'. Nor was he allowed a private audience; his absence from Court at a time of pressing pastoral need having distanced him from the royal confidence and strengthened Dudley's hold. Cranmer was also as naïve as Edward himself in supposing that a shift in the succession could endure any longer than it would take the Lady Mary to get to London. In matters of *haut politique* lawful authority inevitably took priority over divisions in doctrine. The bookish primate, more than usually out of touch with a deteriorating political situation, was faced with a desperate situation and effectively forced to sign against his better judgement. His use of the pen, however much it calmed the anxieties of a dying boy making ready to meet his Maker, was to make the archbishop appear a gambler whose hand had not this time committed scholarly *marginalia* to paper, but rather had set down an ineradicable mark of hostility to Mary that would inevitably determine his fate.

By signing the 'device for the succession', Cranmer had chosen to obey royal authority rather than heed the promptings of his conscience, but by this date his respect for Royal Supremacy was deeply founded and almost reverential. As for Mary, however much the new queen deplored the constitutional settlement that had served to destroy her mother and repudiate her religion, she was obliged to abide by it for the time being; she did so until December 1554. Against her better judgement Mary thus heeded the emperor, allowing her half-brother a Prayer-Book funeral. In fact Edward gained something of a double send-off, for simultaneously with the funeral, Gardiner celebrated requiem Mass in the chapel of the Tower 'with his mitre on ... after the old popish form' (Strype). Cranmer conducted the Westminster Abbey service, the quaint record of Julius Terentianus informing John ab Ulmis that this was done 'in English, or in a christian way, with many tears'. Otherwise, once he with the rest of the Council had acknowledged Mary as queen, the archbishop went to ground at Lambeth.

But this was not for long, for Cranmer's silence was soon misinterpreted as no mere acceptance of the accession, but as actual approval of the newly-restored Mass. When his own suffragan - Bishop Thornden of Dover - offered the traditional sacrifice in Cranmer's Cathedral Church at Canterbury, two options faced the primate: acquiescence or repudiation. Although he may well have hoped that the Council would take the initiative, enabling him to learn precisely where he stood with Queen Mary, it was Cranmer's letter of denial (making it clear that he had decidedly not set up the Mass again) and denunciation, printed and placarded far and wide, that precipitated action. In law, the archbishop's action was not seditious because the mass itself remained illegal. Nevertheless, Cranmer's repudiation of Thornden as a 'false, flattering, and lying monk', and reference to rumours that he had himself offered, 'to say mass before the queen's highness at Paul's, or in any other place, I never did it as her grace well knoweth' must have drawn unwelcome attention to him[**Extract 1**].

For his guilt in the proclamation of the Lady Jane Grey, the Council sent Cranmer to the Tower on 13 September 1553. Tried for treason two months later, the archbishop was convicted, and his attainder confirmed by Parliament. Nor was his absence from the block in February 1554 an indication of mercy; it was merely a sign of exemplary punishment to come. Being altogether loathed by Mary, Cranmer had no hope of a royal pardon despite an abject plea of penitent apology. He acknowledged her to be 'christian queen and governor', and his letter not only recounts the dilemma Dudley's 'device' had posed for him as primate, but also contrasts the role of godly prince with that of private subjects, whose duty it is 'quietly to suffer that they cannot amend'[**Extract 2**].

Cranmer spent over six months in the Tower of London. In early March 1554, the Council ordered him, with Bishops Ridley and Latimer, to be taken to Oxford, but it was April before Bocardo, the town gaol there, received them. The time may have passed rapidly enough for a queen and Council burdened with preparations for the

Spanish marriage and frustrated by Wyatt's insurrection, but for his part Cranmer must have found the delay peculiarly depressing. With Gardiner's star in the ascendant again, he immersed himself in ever-intensive study of the Eucharist to make ready for public disputation. It was Lent, but the penitential season was unexpectedly relieved and Cranmer's morale boosted when congenial fellowship came his way as a result of Wyatt's rising. As Ridley wrote to Grindal:

> ... it chanced by reason of the tumult stirred up in Kent, there was so many prisoners in the Tower, that my Lord of Canterbury, Mr Latimer, Mr Bradford, and I, were put all together in one prison, where we remained still almost to the next Easter. *Ridley*, p. 390

The Guildhall treason trial of 1553 had shown Cranmer in a poor light, his change of plea affording historians at least an indication that the archbishop entertained some reservations about unquestioning obedience to the godly prince. At Oxford his disputation before the universities proved equally unimpressive, largely because the prisoner found himself in ignorance of the form the proceedings were to take. Solemnly charged before thirty-three robed commissioners assembled to meet him in the Church of St Mary the Virgin, Cranmer was treated rather like Luther before the imperial Diet at Worms. For after being faced with articles framed to highlight his heresy - he was obliged to subscribe to the real presence and the sacrifice propitiatory of the Mass - Cranmer had to withdraw and submit in writing an opinion to be debated the following week. Moreover, when that debate took place, on Monday, 16 April 1554, the Dean of Westminster as Prolocutor prefaced the proceedings by announcing the aim of the commission to be the refutation of heresy. Effectively denied the opportunity of genuine debate, Cranmer thus became the object of carping criticism in an often unruly six-hour ordeal, his letter of complaint to the Council recording what must have been the anti-climax of a lifetime [**Extract 3**].

Back in Bocardo, Cranmer was now an excommunicate heretic. Yet many months had to pass before the authorities were able to move in for the kill. Such a final solution had to have the full force of law; the queen and her advisers realising that until the English schism was healed and papal authority restored, Cranmer could suffer no more than humiliation. Political caution and diplomatic complexity delayed these proceedings, and it was not until 30 November that Reginald, Cardinal Pole, used legatine authority formally to declare before Parliament the end of the breach with Rome. Even so, a landowning interest that had benefited from monastic dissolutions still needed reassurance about the scale of the Catholic programme. Revival of heresy laws was one thing, the return of monastic spoils quite another. Accordingly, when Caraffa, at the outset of his pontificate as Paul IV, condemned the alienation and theft of Church land and other property, Pole shrewdly and skilfully secured an extension of the exemption granted in respect of England by Pope Julius III. Needless to state, Pole found the English Church in a bad way; visitations revealed a sad situation with many cures in charge of priests whose principal concern had been not so much for their flock as to stay in office by facing both ways. With so much to be done then, it was particularly unfortunate that an obsession with traditional orthodoxy compelled Mary to proceed at once with the extirpation of heresy. She was in no shadow of doubt that such a policy should have absolute priority.

Against this background, it may seem surprising that Cranmer continued to languish in gaol. No doubt with the realisation that once deprived, the archbishop of Canterbury would have to be replaced, the Council cooled its heels. However, in March 1555 an application went to Rome to secure a special commission that could try the man who had, after all, been duly appointed Primate of All England by the pope in the first place. A six-month delay ensued, but continued study kept Cranmer constant in the convictions that had pleased many in the 1554 disputation. During that debate, he had referred to Marcus Antonius; this was the pseudonym used by Gardiner when he wrote the *Confutation* of Cranmer's *Answer*, a work the bishop of Winchester had published at Paris in 1552 when he was himself detained in the Tower. Lodged in Bocardo, Cranmer certainly concerned himself with eucharistic doctrine. A letter of November 1555, written to a lawyer engaged to draw up an appeal to a General Council of the Church, makes reference to 'mine answer against Marcus Antonius Constantius, which I have now in hand', and suggests that from prison Cranmer was preparing a counter-attack which, if it did not see the light of day in published form, must marvellously have concentrated its author's mind as he awaited trial.

If papal process gave the archbishop the customary eighty-day citation to appear in Rome, only five days after the writ had been served on him, Cranmer was brought from Bocardo (12 September 1555) to face Brokes, bishop of Gloucester and sub-delegate to Jacopo, Cardinal Puteo, Caraffa's Inquisitor General. The trial itself began on 30 September, the archbishop being obliged to answer sixteen articles. Covering the full spectrum of his ecclesiastical ministry and private life, these charged Cranmer in such a way that correctly to answer his interrogator, he had to give affirmative replies which, once uttered, amounted to admissions of guilt. In drafting these articles, the Curia wielded a secret weapon that devastated the defendant, not least because his memory was weighed down with the scriptural and patristic 'proofs' he had long been preparing to use in debating the high matter of the sacrament with his adversaries. The interrogation, set out together with the archbishop's answers as *Processus contra Cranmerum*, clearly shows how the defendant was cut down to size to establish, at least for the court, his heretical pravity [**Extract 4**].

By serving Henry VIII, Cranmer had consistently opposed the papal supremacy. Yet as proctor for Philip and Mary, Dr Thomas Martin devastated the archbishop with the charge that he had broken his sacred oath of consecration. For here was a lawful Tudor regime that had repudiated the supremacy Cranmer believed to be firmly founded in scripture and tradition. Confused at the very thought, the archbishop was soon routed when Martin catechised him about the conscientious qualifications he had troubled to make before taking his oath to the Pope in 1533. Evidence of such perjury in a high-ranking prelate in no way impressed his hearers; and before Cranmer recovered his composure, Martin dared to taunt him on his own holy ground, and scored again when the archbishop had to admit making changes in his eucharistic understanding, which made him seem a trifler. Finally, the penetrating proctor returned to the supremacy issue, his relentless logic leading Cranmer on in much the same way as Eck had led Luther when he triumphed over the reformer at Leipzig. For if Henry VIII had been head of the Church, as Cranmer readily agreed, what of Nero? [**Extract 5**].

Back in Bocardo, Cranmer had every reason to feel depressed. Duly attested by notaries present with Brokes, and by the royal proctors Martin and Story at the St Mary's trial, the documents had gone to Rome. The verdict was not in doubt, for all charges were declared proven; but according to canon law papal authority alone could deprive Cranmer of the archbishopric, and the English authorities were determined to go by the book. Then too, Latimer and Ridley had gone to the stake on 16 October. Latimer's enduring 'candle' sermon apart, it had been an unusually vile affair, Ridley's slow and smouldering fire consuming only his legs, to leave him conscious and in screaming agony until his end finally came. Although legal formalities imposed a technical delay on the authorities, it is hard to avoid the conclusion that the pyre was intended to shock Cranmer into submission. A counselling session with Friar Pedro de Soto prevented the archbishop taking leave of his brethren, yet he was nevertheless obliged to view their execution from the prison roof.

Having thus been made fully aware of what to expect from the authorities - for Marian orthodoxy was not to be deflected by heretical pleading - Cranmer chose precisely this moment to write a remarkable *apologia pro vita sua* to the queen. His refusal to recognise the bishop of Gloucester at his trial, he explained, stemmed from conviction that 'the pope's authority . . . repugneth to the crown imperial of this realm'. Death itself could not therefore grieve him more 'than to have my most dread and most gracious sovereign lord and lady (to whom under God I do owe all obedience) to be mine accusers in judgement within their own realm, before any stranger and outward power'. Nor did his explanation rest there, for Cranmer used the supremacy issue to introduce and justify to the godly prince the whole range of his ministry as a reformer. Mary was thus treated to the archbishop's analysis of services rendered to the English Church under her late father and brother. Cranmer stressed his concern that 'all christian people ... diligently learn God's word'; and then proceeded to justify vernacular worship and the *Book of Common Prayer* in consequence. Preaching, communion in both kinds, a further repudiation of papal authority, and one of his clearest expositions of the [Swiss] eucharistic presence, were all justified in turn before his peroration deplored Brokes's perjury in taking 'his bishoprick both of the queen's majesty and of the pope, making to each of them a solemn oath' [**Extract 6**].

Such correspondence should be seen in the wider context of the archbishop's recantations, for together with another significant letter intended to make Queen Mary aware of the conflicting nature of the oaths taken at her coronation, it clearly indicates Cranmer's conviction about and growing obsession with the doctrine of the godly prince [**Extract 7**]. In short, well before he was confronted with the intolerable pressures soon to be placed upon him, the archbishop was determined to defend his adherence to the consistent principle that removal of the papal headship had made possible such reformation of the English Church as he had achieved. Accordingly, should the queen permit, he was ready in person to confront the rejected Roman authority, a suggestion clearly rooted more in missionary fervour than rational conviction: 'as for mine appearance at Rome, if your majesty will give me leave, I will appear there: and I trust that God shall put in my mouth to defend his truth there as well as here'.

In Rome, needless to state, once the prescribed period had passed, Paul IV himself excommunicated Cranmer, bell, book and candle (on 4 December 1555). The contumacious clerk was to be deprived of Canterbury's ecclesiastical dignity and degraded from holy orders according to precise curial procedures before being transferred to secular authority for execution. In England, meanwhile, the queen had forwarded Cranmer's letter to Pole; and that legate, shortly to be presented to the now vacant primatial see, sent his imprisoned predecessor a singularly unsympathetic reply. But in Oxford, Alice, Cranmer's sister, had arrived to argue for her brother's rights. In this she was singularly successful, and not only gained his temporary release from Bocardo, but determinedly used her training as a nun to encourage her brother back towards orthodoxy during December and the early New Year. This was a peaceful interlude, but it was to have cruel consequences - for dinners with the Dean and the sporting diversion of bowls on the lawns of Christ Church doubtless brought with them nostalgia for donnish routines of his own in Cambridge days. There were even discussions of a theological nature: Juan de Garcina, the Spanish friar, newly appointed Regius Professor of Divinity, continuing, where Alice Cranmer left off, to prepare the patient for recantation.

Massive frustration followed, however; for once the papal judgement was known in England, Cranmer, as a leprous excommunicate, was cast once again into the outer darkness of Bocardo. If the manifest injustice of his situation was in time to break him, initially at least it stirred Cranmer to complete, with the assistance of an Oxford lawyer, a dignified appeal to a General Council of the Church on the ground that no pope could act impartially in his own cause. A lengthy but little-known document, Cranmer's appeal 'from the Pope, to the next General Council' contains a number of passages that deserve to be more widely known [**Extract 8**].

Not that there was the remotest chance of such a plea achieving the desired end, particularly once the bishops of Ely and London had arrived in Oxford to conduct the degradation ceremony demanded by Caraffa in accordance with the process laid down in *Pontificale Romanum*. And so, on St Valentine's Day no less, Cranmer was brought before Thirlby and Bonner in the choir of the cathedral for the humiliation that popes deemed appropriate for those who defied their supremacy over Christ's Church. In the judgement of A.F. Pollard, 'The procedure on such occasions was a monument of exquisite cruelty; nothing that ingenuity could devise was omitted to abuse the victim and wound his spirit.' To make matters worse, if that were possible, the belligerent Bonner used the occasion to get even with Cranmer, a number of old grudges prompting him openly to mock the archbishop who had been instrumental in replacing him, by translating Ridley from Rochester to London, in Edward's reign.

When consecrated and installed as archbishop in 1533, Cranmer would have been fully vested; and what was then memorable was now to be made unmentionable. As Foxe wrote, 'Then they invested him in all manner of robes of a bishop and archbishop . . . every thing . . . most rich and costly.' But now 'every thing in this was of canvas and old clouts, with a mitre and pall of the same suit done upon him in mockery' (*A & M*, Vol. VIII, p. 72). First, he was degraded *ab ordine archiepiscopali*; interestingly he protested loudly when the symbolic pallium was stripped from his back. Conferred by the pope, or sent from Rome whenever a primate was consecrated, this seal of papal favour and supremacy a consistent Cranmer might have been pleased to relinquish; that he was not serves to underline the mental anguish of the man, a tension certainly heightened by his conviction of Bonner's own unworthiness for such high office. Then the chalice and paten that had been placed in his hands were snatched from Cranmer, his priestly vestments being likewise removed to indicate that he had forfeited all power to offer the Christian sacrifice for the living and the dead. Next, he was degraded from the orders of deacon and sub-deacon, the gospels and epistles were taken from his hands, and the tunic and stole were stripped from his body. And finally, after suffering similar indignities related to the loss of status associated with the minor orders of acolyte and exorcist, reader and doorkeeper (*ostiaratus*), the commissioners even concerned themselves with vestiges of the heretic's tonsure and annointing. Foxe wrote:

> Then a barber clipped his hair round about, and the bishop scraped the tops of his fingers where he had been anointed, wherein bishop Bonner behaved himself as roughly and unmannerly, as the other bishop was to him soft and gentle.
>
> *A & M*, Vol. VIII, p. 79.

By the charade of counter-liturgy, England's liturgical genius was thus repudiated. If there was a climax to the proceedings, it came when

Cranmer handed Thirlby his appeal, although that was, of course, immediately disallowed. At the last, too, the archbishop who had made loud protest when his pallium had been removed ignored Bonner's 'now you are no lord any more' with the resignation described by the sympathetic Foxe:

'All this' quoth the archbishop, 'needed not; I had myself done with this gear long ago'. Last of all they stepped him out of his gown into his jacket, and put upon him a poor yeoman-beadle's gown, full bare and nearly worn, and as evil favourably made, as one might lightly see, and a townsman's cap on his head; and so delivered him to the secular power.

Foxe clearly used such artistic exactitude to parallel the indignities suffered by Christ, his homespun style moving the reader to pity the plight of Cranmer. But there the comparison ends, for both before and after the events of 14 February 1556, the erstwhile archbishop penned brief but poignant recantations. The first of these, acknowledging that Mary and Philip had 'received the pope's authority' was straightforward deference to the judgement of the godly prince, albeit recalling the qualifying formula used in reverse when for their *praemunire* Henry VIII had secured from the English clergy the historic submission of 1531. Cranmer was thus prepared, 'to take the pope for chief head of this church of England, so far as God's laws and the laws and customs of the realm will permit'. The second, containing no such reservations, was notable for a brevity that made it altogether unacceptable - not that the queen and the Privy Council sought Cranmer's recantation: their objective was his execution, although there were some who hoped for both and realised that a full recantation by Cranmer must irreparably damage the heretics and their cause. A third submission (none of Cranmer's statements sufficiently repudiated 'the new religion' to indicate the complete repudiation of conviction consonant with *recantation*) followed, Cranmer indicating his willingness to observe royal and papal authority and to send his work on the Eucharist for assessment by a General Council. Then, bullied by Bonner on 16 February, Cranmer wrote a general statement of belief 'in all articles and points of the christian religion and catholic faith, as the catholic church doth believe, and hath ever believed from the beginning'. He made no mention of Rome nor of the pope, and in that sense almost mocked in his bewildered insecurity the man who two days before had taken such savage delight in his degradation.

Once back in London, Bonner reported to Mary, and his account must have convinced her that Cranmer's submissions were not to be trusted. The next move was that Philip and Mary issued to the mayor and bailiffs of Oxford the writ for 'the execution of Thomas, late archbishop of Canterburye' leaving the date to be determined [**Extract 9**]. Cranmer was not immediately made aware of this; he was undergoing concentrated brain-washing sessions which Friar Juan de Garcina and Canon Sidall calculated would prompt from him both penitence and a convincing recantation. Whether they offered their pathetic prisoner the promise of retreat into private life with his books as solace will never be known. For if the source material of *Bishop Cranmer's Recantacyons* has countered much of John Foxe's narrative, there is a grim shroud here that barely conceals the torture chamber. Only by such means indeed could the fifth submission, a thorough recantation of the principal reforming ideals that had motivated Cranmer's developing ministry, have been procured [**Extract 10**].

When news of this capitulation reached them, the authorities determined to concentrate their advantage. Dudley's contemptible cowardice at the block had already done much to discredit the Protestant cause, and if Cranmer's evident lack of balance could also be exploited, it would go a long way to boost 'the old religion' in the popular mind. At the same time, neither mercy nor forgiveness were to be extended, Mary being fully determined to make the arch-heretic abjure in an even more abject manner than Dudley had. At Oxford the formidable five - Friars Pedro de Soto and Juan de Garcina (the Regius Professors of Hebrew and Divinity), Dean Marshall, Canon Sidall and the Friar Roscius - worked hard for their penitent's soul, the mental anguish of the man easing their task. *Bishop Cranmer's Recantacyons* relates a terrible dream sequence, like a kind of doom painting, that disturbed Cranmer at the last. In what must have been a nightmarish situation, this afforded the prisoner a startling vision of rival kings competing for his immortal soul. In the circumstances there was perhaps nothing unusual about this, save that this was no obvious contest between God and the Devil, but rather between Christ and Henry VIII! The historian cannot cross such Freudian frontiers, and A.F. Pollard was properly sceptical of the *Recantacyons* as a source for 'Cranmer's last days'. Nevertheless, that the prisoner in Bocardo was finally broken on the rack of undue deference to the 'godly prince' is not in doubt, and, terribly alone in the depths of despair and the inevitable mood of accompanying depression, it must have been a relatively simple matter for Roscius to force on Cranmer that most damning of recantations [**Extract 11**].

Speculation is no part of the historical discipline, and, no doubt for this reason, Cranmer has been almost as roughly handled by Clio and her disciples, as by those who tortured him in the first place. And tortured he must have been. First of all, for a persistent friar, and catspaw of the Regius Professor of Divinity, to presume to indoctrinate the one-time primate in matters eucharistic - even to the point of securing attendance at Mass - must rank as an act of mental cruelty. Secondly, a cursory glance at the sixth recantation indicates from the internal evidence of both style and substance that it could not have been composed by Cranmer had he been in his right mind, and accordingly that it was under extreme duress that such a submission was obtained. The principal objections to its authenticity relate to the complex analogy made with the robber on the cross. Just as the thief crucified with Christ could not return his ill-gotten gains, so Cranmer by abusing his office and authority had 'deprived both Christ of respect and the realm of faith and religion'. The robber could not make reparation because he was nailed to the Roman gibbet, but his tongue - the one free member of his suffering body - not only expressed loathing of his wretched way of life, but also, by confessing the innocence of the crucified Christ, gained forgiveness of sins and entry to paradise. The recantation implies that Cranmer might not be so fortunate, and an obscure allusion to an Old Testament prophet (Hosea 14: 2) offers the sacrifice of his lips as all that is left to an arch-heretic 'deserving of every not merely human and temporal, but divine and eternal punishment'. Cranmer was thus the cause and originator of the 'divorce', just as the 'divorce' was 'the seed-bed of all the woes and disasters of this realm'. The resulting schism was his sole responsibility. He it was, moreover, who 'created a huge opening for all heresies' to insult the Eucharist and, in a book on the sacrament, prove himself a worse persecutor than both Saul and the crucified thief to rank as 'the most wicked of all the earth has ever borne'. The charge relates to Cranmer's sin against heaven, because he has deprived his people of their true destiny by denying them of 'supersubstantial food' in the sacrament. The very words are as remote from the range of vocabulary used by so superb a stylist as the peroration of the piece is from Cranmer's grasp of Christian doctrine. For at the end, the pathetic penitent is made to plead that 'the highest pontiff' grant him pardon 'for the sake of Christ's clemency for offences committed against him and his apostolic seat' - a petition that could not have been penned by the author of the 'Homily of Salvation'. Truly, even if Cranmer's life began with intimidation at the hands of an 'over-severe scholemaster', the brow-beating he received from Roscius in these last days must have devastated so sensitive a spirit in his old age.

Henry Cole reached Oxford by Wednesday, 18 March. Appointed by the queen to preach at the execution, he visited Bocardo to break the news that the burning would take place on the following Saturday, 21 March 1556. Although Roscius had already made Cranmer write out the devastating piece that Roscius himself undoubtedly phrased, which was actually signed on the same fateful Wednesday. Not that even this satisfied the inquisitors, who now informed Cranmer that, to be acceptable, public satisfaction must follow private confession; and in the time that remained he duly set about preparing drafts of the broadsheet, 'The Prayer and Saying of Thomas Cranmer, a little before his death', to be published by John Cawood with the Council's authority.

The tragedy of Cranmer's final situation is too well-known to need to be rehearsed here. Suffice it to state that, whatever conflicts of evidence have faced scholars over the detailed timetable of humiliation forced on him at the end, the last-minute brilliance of recanting his very recantation both devastated his enemies and provided the courage for that ultimate gesture of defiance in the fire [**Extract 12**].

Extract 1

As the devil, Christ's ancient adversary, is a liar and the father of lying, even so he hath ever stirred up his servants and members to persecute Christ and his true word and religion, which lying he feareth not to do most earnestly at this present. For whereas a prince of most famous memory, king Henry the Eighth, seeing the great abuses of the Latin mass, reformed some things therein in time; and after, our late sovereign lord Edward the Sixth took the same wholly away for the manifold errors and abuses thereof, and restored in the place thereof Christ's holy supper according to Christ's institution, and as the apostles in the primitive church used the same in the beginning: now goeth the devil about by lying to overthrow the Lord's holy supper again, and to restore his Latin satisfactory mass, a thing of his own invention and device. And to bring the same the more easily to pass, some of his inventors have abused the name of me, Thomas archbishop of Canterbury, bruiting abroad that I have set up the mass again in Canterbury, and that I offered myself to say mass at the burial of our late sovereign prince king Edward the Sixth, and also that I offered myself to say mass before the queen's highness at Paul's church in London, and I wot not where. And although I have been well exercised these xx years in suffering and bearing evil bruits, reports, and lies, and have not been much grieved thereat, but have borne all things quietly; yet when untrue reports and lies turn to the hinderance of God's truth, then are they in no wise tolerate or to be suffered. Wherefore this is to signify to the world, that it was not I that did set up the mass in Canterbury, but it was a false, flattering, and lying monk, with a dozen of his blind adherents, which caused the mass to be set up there, and that without mine advise or counsel.

A Declaration of the Reverend Father in Christ, Thomas Archbishop of Canterbury, concerning the untrue report and slander of some, which reported, that he should set up again the mass in Canterbury; in Cranmer I, *pp. 428-9.*

Extract 2

Most lamentably mourning and moaning himself unto your highness, Thomas Cranmer, although unworthy either to write or speak unto your highness, yet having no person that I know to be mediator for me, and knowing your pitiful ears ready to hear all pitiful complaints, and seeing so many before to have felt your abundant clemency in like case, am now constrained most lamentably, and with most penitent and sorrowful heart, to ask mercy and pardon for my heinous folly and offence, in consenting and following the testament and last will of our late sovereign lord king Edward VI your grace's brother: which will, God he knoweth, I never liked; nor never anything grieved me so much that your grace's brother did. And if by any means it had been in me to have letted the making of that will, I would have done it. And what I said therein, as well to the council as to himself, divers of your majesty's council can report: but none so well as the marquis of Northampton, and the lord Darcy, then lord chamberlain to the king's majesty; which two were present at the communication between the king's majesty and me. I desired to talk with the king's majesty alone, but I could not be suffered, and so I failed of my purpose. For if I might have communed with the king alone, and at good leisure, my trust was, that I should have altered him from that purpose; but, they being present, my labour was in vain.

Then when I could not dissuade him from the said will, and both he and his privy council also informed me that the judges and his learned counsel said, that the act of entailing the crown, made by his father, could not be prejudical to him, but that he, being in possession of the crown, might make his will thereof; this seemed very strange unto me; but being the sentence of the judges, and other his learned counsel in the laws of this realm (as both he and his council informed me), methought it became not me, being unlearned in the law, to stand against my prince therein. And so at length I was required by the king's majesty himself to set to my hand to his will; saying, that he trusted that I alone would not be more repugnant to his will than the rest of the council were: (which words surely grieved my heart very sore) and so I granted him to subscribe his will, and to follow the same. Which when I had set my hand unto, I did it unfeignedly and without dissimulation.

For the which I submit myself most humbly unto your majesty, acknowledging mine offence with most grievous and sorrowful heart, and beseeching your mercy and pardon: which my heart giveth me shall not be denied unto me, being granted before to so many, which travailed not so much to dissuade both the king and his council as I did.

And whereas it is contained in two acts of parliament (as I understand), that I, with the duke of Northumberland, should devise and compass the deprivation of your majesty from your royal crown, surely it is untrue. For the duke never opened his mouth to me, to move me any such matter, nor I him; nor his heart was not such toward me (seeking long time my destruction), that he would either trust me in such matter, or think that I would be persuaded by him. It was other of the council that moved me, and the king himself, the duke of Northumberland not being present. Neither before, neither after, had I ever any privy communication with the duke of that matter, saving that openly at the council-table the duke said unto me, that it became not me to say to the king as I did, when I went about to dissuade him from the said will . . . .

Cranmer to Queen Mary (1553); in *Cranmer II*, pp. 442-4.

Extract 3

. . . this is to signify unto your lordships, that upon Monday, Tuesday, and Wednesday last past were open disputations here in Oxford against me, master Ridley, and master Latimer, in three matters concerning the sacrament: first, of the real presence: secondly, of transubstantiation: and thirdly, of the sacrifice of the mass. How the other two were used, I cannot tell; for we were separated: so that none of us knew what the other said, nor how they were ordered. But as concerning myself, I can report, that I never knew nor heard of a more confused disputation in all my life. For albeit there was one appointed to dispute against me, yet every man spake his mind, and brought forth what him liked without order. And such haste was made, that no answer could be suffered to be given fully to any argument, before another brought a new argument. And in such weighty and large matters there was no remedy, but the disputations must needs be ended in one day, which can scantly well be ended in three months. And when we had answered them, then they would not appoint us one day to bring forth our proofs, that they might answer us again, being required of me thereunto: whereas I myself have more to say, than can be well discussed in twenty days. The means to resolve the truth had been, to have suffered us to answer fully to all that they could say, and then they again to answer to all that we could say. But why they would not answer us, what other cause can there be, but that either they feared the matter, that they were not able to answer us; or else (as by their haste might well appear) they came, not to speak the truth, but to condemn us in post haste, before the truth might be thoroughly tried and heard? for in all haste we were all three condemned of heresy upon Friday. Thus much I thought good to signify unto your lordships, that you may know the indifferent handling of matters, leaving the judgement thereof unto your wisdoms. And I beseech your lordships to remember me, a poor prisoner, unto the queen's majesty; and I shall pray, as I do daily, unto God for the long preservation of your lordships in all godliness and felicity.

Cranmer to the Lords of the Council, 23 April 1554; in *Cranmer II*, pp. 445-6.

Extract 4

1. *Interrog.* First was objected, and he, the foresaid Thomas Cranmer, being yet free, and before he entered into holy orders, married one Joan, surnamed black, or brown, dwelling at the sign of the Dolphin, in Cambridge.

Answ. Whereunto he answered, that whether she was called black, or brown he knew not; but that he married there one Joan, that he granted.

2. *Interrog.* That, after the death of the foresaid wife, he entered into holy orders, and after that was made archbishop by the pope.

Answ. He received (he said) a certain bull of the pope, which he delivered unto the king, and was archbishop by him.

3. *Interrog.* Item, that he, being in holy orders, married another

woman, as his second wife, named Anne; and so was twice married.

Answ. To this he granted.

4. *Interrog.* Item, in the time of king Henry the eighth he kept the said wife secretly, and had children by her.

Answ. Hereunto he also granted; affirming that it was better for him to have his own, than to do like other priests, holding and keeping other men's wives.

5. *Interrog.* Item, in the time of king Edward he brought out the said his wife openly, affirming and professing publicly the same to be his wife.

Answ. he denied not but he so did, and lawfully might do the same, forasmuch as the laws of the realm did so permit him. . . .

12. *Interrog.* Item, that he was and is notoriously infamed with the note of schism, as who not only himself receded from the catholic church and see of Rome, but also moved the king and subjects of this realm to the same.

Answ. As touching the receding, that he well granted; but that receding or departing (said he) was only from the see of Rome, and had in it no matter of any schism.

13. *Interrog.* Item, that he had been twice sworn to the pope - And withal Dr Martin brought out the instrument of the public notary, wherein was contained his protestation made when he should be consecrated, asking if he had any thing else protested.

Answ. Whereunto he answered, that he did nothing but by the laws of the realm.

14. *Interrog.* Item, that he, the said archbishop of Canterbury, did not only offend in the premises, but also in taking upon him the authority of the see of Rome, in that, without leave or licence from the said see, he consecrated bishops and priests.

Answ. He granted that he did execute such things as were wont to be referred to the pope, at what time it was permitted to him by the public laws and determination of the realm.

15. *Interrog.* Item, that when the whole realm had subscribed to the authority of the pope, he only still persisted in his error.

Answ. That he did not admit the pope's authority, he confessed to be true: but that he erred in the same, that he denied.

Extract 5

Martin: Now, sir, as touching the last part of your oration, you denied that the pope's holiness was supreme head of the church of Christ.

Cranmer: I did so.

Martin: Who say you then is supreme head?

Cranmer: Christ.

Martin: But whom hath Christ left here in earth his vicar and head of his church?

Cranmer: Nobody.

Martin: Ah! why told you not Henry this, when you made him supreme head? and now nobody is. This is treason against his own person, as you then made him.

Cranmer: I mean not but every king in his own realm and dominion is supreme head, and so was he supreme head of the church of Christ in England.

Martin: Is this always true? and was it ever so in Christ's church?

Cranmer: It was so.

Martin: Then what say you by Nero? He was the mightiest prince of the earth, after Christ was ascended. Was he head of Christ's church?

Cranmer: Nero was Peter's head.

Martin: I ask, whether Nero was head of the church, or no? If he were not, it is false that you said before, that all princes be, and ever were, heads of the church within their realms.

Cranmer: Nay, it is true, for Nero was head of the church, that is, in worldly respect of the temporal bodies of men, of whom the church consisteth; for so he beheaded Peter and the apostles. And the Turk too is head of the church of Turkey.

Martin: Then he that beheaded the heads of the church, and crucified the apostles, was head of Christ's church; and he that was never member of the church, is head of the church, by your new found understanding of God's word.

From the Examination at Oxford before Brokes, September 1555; in *Cranmer II*, p. 219.

Extract 6

... whereas our Saviour Christ ordained the sacrament of his most precious body and blood to be received of all christian people under the forms of both body and wine, and said of the cup, 'Drink ye all of this'; the pope giveth a clean contrary commandment, that no lay-man shall drink of the cup of their salvation; as though the cup of salvation by the blood of Christ pertained not to lay-men. And whereas Theophilus Alexandrinus (whose works St Jerome did translate about eleven hundred years past) saith, 'That if Christ had been crucified for the devils, his cup should not be denied them'; yet the pope denieth the cup of Christ to christian people, for whom Christ was crucified. So that if I should obey the pope in these things, I must needs disobey my Saviour Christ.

But I was answered hereunto (as commonly the papists do answer), that under the form of bread is whole Christ's flesh and blood: so that whosoever receiveth the form of bread, receiveth as well Christ's blood as his flesh. Let it be so: yet in the form of bread only Christ's blood is not drunken, but eaten; nor is it received in the cup in the form of wine, as Christ commanded, but eaten with the flesh under the form of bread. And, moreover, the bread is not the sacrament of his blood, but of his flesh only; nor the cup is not the sacrament of his flesh, but of his blood only. And so the pope keepeth from all lay-persons the sacrament of their redemption by Christ's blood, which Christ commandeth to be given unto them.

And furthermore, Christ ordained the sacrament in two kinds, the one separated from the other, to be a representation of his death, where his blood was separated from his flesh; which is not represented in one kind alone: so that the lay people receive not the whole sacrament, whereby Christ's death is represented, as he commanded.

Moreover, as the pope taketh upon him to give the temporal sword, or royal and imperial power, to kings and princes; so doth he likewise take upon him to depose them from their imperial states, if they be disobedient to him, and commandeth the subjects to disobey their princes, assoiling the subjects as well of their obedience as of their lawful oaths made unto their true kings and princes, directly contrary to God's commandment, who commandeth all subjects to obey their kings, or their rulers under them. . . .

Wherefore, seeing the pope thus (to overthrow both God's laws and man's laws) taketh upon him to make emperors and kings to be vassals and subjects unto him, and specially the crown of this realm, with the laws and customs of the same; I see no mean how I may consent to admit his usurped power within this realm, contrary to mine oath, mine obedience to God's law, mine allegiance and duty to your majesty, and my love and affection to this realm.

This that I have spoken against the power and authority of the pope, I have not spoken (I take God to record and judge) for any malice I owe to the pope's person, whom I know not; but I shall pray to God to give him grace that he may seek above all things to promote God's honour and glory, and not to follow the trade of his predecessors in these latter days.

Nor have I spoken it for fear of punishment, and to avoid the same, thinking it rather an occasion to aggravate than to diminish my trouble: but I have spoken it for my most bounden duty to the crown, liberties, laws, and customs of this realm of England; but most specially to discharge my conscience in uttering the truth to God's glory . . .

And as touching the sacrament, I said: forasmuch as the whole matter standeth in the understanding of these words of Christ, 'This is my body, This is my blood'; I said that Christ in these words made demonstration of the bread and wine, and spake figuratively, calling bread his body and wine his blood, because he ordained them to be sacraments of his body and blood. And where the papists say in these two points contrary unto me, that Christ called not bread his body, but a substance uncertain, nor spake figuratively: herein I said I would be judged by the old church and which doctrine could be proved the elder, that I would stand unto. And forasmuch as I have alleged in my book many old authors, both Greeks and Latins, which above a thousand years after Christ continually taught as I do; if they could bring forth but one old author, that saith in these two points as they say, I offered six or seven years ago, and do offer yet still, that I will give place unto them. . . .

For in the beginning the church of Rome taught a pure and sound doctrine of the sacrament. But after that the church of Rome fell into a new doctrine of transubstantiation; with the doctrine they changed the use of the sacrament, contrary to that Christ commanded, and the old church of Rome used above a thousand years. And yet, to deface the old, they say that the new is the old: wherein for my part I am content to stand to the trial. But their doctrine is so fond and uncomfortable that I marvel that any man would allow it, if he knew what it is. But, howsoever they bear the people in hand, that which they write in their books hath neither truth nor comfort.

For by their doctrine, of one body of Christ is made two bodies; one natural, having distance of members, with form and proportion of man's perfect body, and this body is in heaven; but the body of Christ in the sacrament, by their own doctrine, must needs be a monstrous body, having neither distance of members, nor form, fashion, or proportion of a man's natural body. And such a body is in the sacrament, teach they, and goeth into the mouth with the form of bread, and entereth no farther than the form of bread goeth, nor tarrieth no longer than the form of bread is by natural heat in digesting: so that when the form of bread is digested, that body of Christ is gone. And forasmuch as evil men be as long in digesting as good men, the body of Christ, by their doctrine, entereth as far and tarrieth as long in wicked men as in godly men. And what comfort can be herein to any christian man, to receive Christ's unshapen body, and it to enter no farther than the stomach, and to depart by and bye as soon as the bread is consumed?

It seemeth to me a more sound and comfortable doctrine, that Christ hath but one body, and that hath form and fashion of a man's true body; which body spiritually entereth into the whole man, body and soul: and though the sacrament be consumed, yet whole Christ remaineth, and feedeth the receiver until eternal life (if he continue in godliness), and never departeth until the receiver forsake him. And as for the wicked, they have not Christ within them at all, who cannot be where Belial is. And this is my faith, and (as meseemeth) a sound doctrine, according to God's word, and sufficient for a Christian to believe in that matter.

[*see also* Chapter 5, Extracts 10 and 11, *above*]

Cranmer to Queen Mary, in a letter of September 1555; *Cranmer II*, pp. 451-4..

Extract 7

I learned by doctor Martin, that at the day of your majesty's coronation you took an oath of obedience to the pope of Rome, and the same time you took another oath to this realm, to maintain the laws, liberties, and customs of the same. And if your majesty did make an oath to the pope, I think it was according to the other oaths which he useth to minister to princes; which is, to be obedient to him, to defend his person, to maintain his authority, honour, laws, lands, and privileges. And if it be so (which I know not but by report), then I beseech your majesty to look upon your oath made to the crown and realm, and to expend and weigh the two oaths together, to see how they do agree, and then to do as your grace's conscience shall give you: for I am surely persuaded that willingly your majesty will not offend, nor do against your conscience for nothing. But I fear me that there be contradictions in your oaths, and that those which should have informed your grace thoroughly, did not their duties therein. And if your majesty ponder the two oaths diligently, I think you shall perceive you were deceived: and then your highness may use the matter as God shall put in your heart. Furthermore, I am kept here from company of learned men, from books, from counsel, from pen and ink, saving at this time to write unto your majesty; which all were necessary for a man being in my case. Wherefore I beseech your majesty, that I may have such of these as may stand with your majesty's pleasure. And as for mine appearance at Rome, if your majesty will give me leave, I will appear there: and I trust that God shall put in my mouth to defend his truth there as well as here. But I refer it wholly to your majesty's pleasure.

Your poor òrator,

T. C.

Cranmer to Queen Mary, from the Tower, in a letter of September 1555; in *Cranmer II*, p. 454.

Extract 8

The law of nature requireth of all men, that so far forth as it may be done without offence to God, every one should seek to defend and preserve his own life. Which thing when I about three days ago bethought myself of, and therewithal remembered how that Martin Luther appealed in his time from pope Leo the X. to a general council (lest I should seem rashly and unadvisedly to cast away myself), I determined to appeal in like sort to some lawful and free general council. But seeing the order and form of an appeal pertaineth to men learned in the law, whereof I myself am ignorant, and seeing that Luther's appeal cometh not to my hand, I proposed to break my mind on this matter to some faithful friend, and skilful in the law, whose help I might use in this behalf; and you only among others came to my remembrance, as a man most meet in this university for my purpose. But this is a matter that requireth great silence, so that no man may know of it before it be done. It is so that I am summoned to make mine answer at Rome the xvi. day of this month: before the which day I think it good, as well as after sentence pronounced, to make mine appeal. But whether I should first appeal from the judge delegate to the pope, and so afterward to the general council, or else, leaving the pope, I should appeal immediately to the council, herein I stand in need of your counsel.

Many causes there be for the which I think good to appeal. First, because I am by an oath bound never to consent to the receiving of the bishop of Rome's authority into this realm. Besides this, whereas I utterly refused to make answer to the articles objected unto me by the bishop of Gloucester, appointed by the pope to be my judge, yet I was content to answer Martin and Story, with this protestation, that mine answer should not be taken as made before a judge, nor yet in place of judgement, but as pertaining nothing to judgement at all; and moreover, after I had made mine answer, I required to have a copy of the same, that I might, either by adding thereunto, or by altering or taking from it, correct and amend it as I thought good: the which though both the bishop of Gloucester, and also the king and queen's proctors, promised me, yet have they altogether broken promise with me, and have not permitted me to correct my said answers according to my request; and yet, notwithstanding, have (as I understand) registered the same as acts formally done in place of judgement.

Finally, forasmuch as all this my trouble cometh upon my departing from the bishop of Rome, and from the popish religion, so that now the quarrel is betwixt the pope himself and me, and no man can be a lawful and indifferent judge in his own cause; it seemeth (methink) good reason that I should be suffered to appeal to some general council in this matter; specially seeing the law of nature (as they say) denieth no man the remedy of appeal in such cases.

Cranmer to a lawyer, November 1555; in *Cranmer II*, pp. 455-6. The appeal itself is printed in the same volume, and after a legal defence, contains three important paragraphs where Cranmer argues for a faith based on scripture and the fathers:

... And touching my doctrine of the sacrament, and other my doctrine, of what kind soever it be, I protest that it was never my mind to write, speak, or understand any thing contrary to the most holy word of God, or else against the holy catholic church of Christ; but purely and simply to imitate and teach those things only, which I had learned of the sacred scripture, and of the holy catholic church of Christ from the beginning, and also according to the exposition of the most holy and learned fathers and martyrs of the church.

And if anything hath peradventure chanced otherwise than I thought, I may err; but heretic I cannot be, forasmuch as I am ready in all things to follow the judgement of the most sacred word of God and of the holy catholic church, desiring none other thing than meekly and gently to be taught, if any where (which God forbid!) I have swerved from the truth.

And I protest and openly confess, that in all my doctrine and preaching, both of the sacrament and of other my doctrine, whatsoever it be, not only I mean and judge those things as the catholic church and the most holy fathers of old, with one accord, have meant and judged; but also I would gladly use the same words that they used, and not use any other words, but to set my hand to all and singular their speeches, phrases, ways, and forms of speech, which they do use in their treatises upon the sacrament, and to keep still their interpretation. But in this thing I only am accused for an heretic, because I allow not the doctrine lately brought in of the sacrament, and because I consent not to words not accustomed in scripture, and unknown to the ancient fathers, but newly invented and brought in by men, and belonging to the destruction of souls, and overthrowing of the pure and old religion.

Cranmer's Appeal at his degradation; in *Cranmer II*, p. 227.

Extract 9

Philip and Mary, by the grace of God, king and queen, to the mayor and bailiff of the city of Oxford, greeting.

Whereas our most holy father Pope Paul, the fourth of his name, has by a sentence pronounced according to the prescript of law sought in that respect and in all respects observed, and judicially and definitively as prescribed by the rules of canon law, judged, declared, pronounced and condemned Thomas Cranmer late archbishop of Canterbury as an heresiarch, anathematised, and manifest heretic, on account of his various heinous manifest errors and damnable heresies, his detestable and vile beliefs, which are opposed and repugnant to our catholic faith and the decision of the universal church, errors which have been by the said Thomas Cranmer in many ways made, committed, stated, affirmed and perpetrated, and publicly and persistently held and defended, and whereas for the same reason the same, our father Pope Paul IV, has by process of law and definitively in prescribed form deprived and stripped the aforesaid Thomas Cranmer of his said archbishopric and other prelacies, ranks, offices and benefices, as we have certain information from him:

And whereas also the reverend fathers in Christ Edmund bishop of London and Thomas bishop of Ely have by the authority of our most holy father the Pope in fact deposed the aforesaid Thomas Cranmer from every order, degree, office and ecclesiastical rank as a proved heretic and heresiarch; as a result of which the same Thomas Cranmer stands at the present time justly, legally and canonically judged to be a heretic and heresiarch, condemned and deposed:

And whereas mother church has nothing further in this respect to do or which should be done against such a rotten and detestable limb and heresiarch, the same reverend fathers have handed over, committed and abandoned the said Thomas Cranmer, convicted heretic and heresiarch, to the arm and power of our secular officers, as is certified by the letters patent of the said reverend fathers indicated by us in our chancellery:

We therefore in our zeal for justice and in defence of the catholic faith, and wishing to maintain and defend the holy church, its rights and liberties, and the catholic faith, to root out and extirpate to the best of our powers heresies and errors of this kind everywhere, and to inflict condign punishment on the aforesaid Thomas, heresiarch, who has been convicted, condemned and deposed: And purposing that a heretic and heresiarch of this kind, who has been in the aforesaid form convicted, condemned and deposed in accordance with the laws and customs of our kingdom of England obtaining in this respect, ought to be burnt at the stake; we command you to have the said Thomas Cranmer, who is in your custody, in a public and open place under the freedom of our said city of Oxford for the aforesaid cause committed to the flames in the presence of the people; and have that Thomas Cranmer actually consumed by that same fire, for a manifest example to other Christians of the detestation in which such crimes are held; and on no account to fail to carry out this order under pain and instant peril, and as you will answer to us thereupon.

Witnessed by ourselves at Westminster on the twenty-fourth day of February in the second and third years of the king and queen.

The Latin original of the writ can be found in *Burnet*, Vol. V. p. 452 (Record XXVII).

Extract 10

I, Thomas Cranmer, anathematize every heresy of Luther and Zwingli and whatsoever dogma is contrary to sound doctrine. But I confess and believe most surely in one holy and catholic visible church, outside which there is no salvation; and I recognize as its supreme head upon earth the Bishop of Rome, whom I admit to be *summus pontifex*, Pope and Vicar of Christ, to whom all the faithful are bound subject. Now as regards the sacraments, I believe in and worship in the sacrament of the Eucharist the true body and blood of Christ, most truly without recourse to any trope or figure of speech contained under the species of bread and wine, the bread being changed and transubstantiated by divine power into the Redeemer's body, and the wine into his blood. And I believe in the other six sacraments (as in this) and hold that which the whole Roman church holds and declares. I believe in addition in a place of purgatory, where for a space are tormented the souls of the departed, for whom the church in holy and salutary fashion

prays, as it also worships the saints and pours out prayers to them. Finally I profess myself in all matters to hold no other opinions than the catholic and Roman church holds; and I regret ever having held and declared any other opinion. But I beg and pray God to deign of his goodness to forgive me the faults I have committed against him and his church; and at the same time I beg and beseech the faithful to pour out prayers for me, and I entreat by the blood of Jesus Christ those who have been led astray by my example or my teaching to return to the unity of the church, so that we may all say the same thing and that there be no schisms among us. Lastly, as I yield myself to Christ's catholic church and its supreme head, so I submit myself to Philip and Mary, sovereigns of England, and to their laws and decrees, and I call almighty God to witness that these admissions have not been made by me to seek anyone's favour or out of fear of anyone, but most freely from the heart, in order to do what is best and take thought for my own conscience, and at the same time for that of others.
By me THOMAS CRANMER
Witnesses of this signature:
Br. John de Villa Garcina
Henry Sidall
Latin text in *Cranmer II*, pp. 563-4.

Extract 11

I, Thomas Cranmer, formerly Archbishop of Canterbury, confess and declare my heartfelt regret that I have most grievously offended against heaven and against the realm of England, or rather the whole of Christ's church, which for a long time I persecuted more savagely than once did Paul, being a blasphemer, persecutor and insulter. Would that I, who surpassed Saul in wickedness and crime, could make useful amends with Paul for the respect which I took away from Christ and the church. But the robber in the Gospel is a solace to my mind. For he then at length came to his senses again, and was then ashamed of robbing, when he could rob no longer; and I (who by the abuse of my office and authority deprived both Christ of respect and this realm of faith and religion) having at length by the goodness of almighty God come to my senses, acknowledge myself the greatest of all sinners, and I desire (if in any way I can) to give full satisfaction first to God, then to the church, and its supreme head, and the sovereigns, and finally to the whole realm of England.

But like that happy robber, when he was unable to restore the money and goods he had stolen (since neither foot nor hand, being nailed to the cross, could perform their function), at least with heart and tongue (which were not tied) declared what the other limbs would have done, had they enjoyed the same freedom as his tongue. With that he confessed Christ innocent, with it he reproved the impudence of his companion, with it he expressed loathing for the life he had lived theretofore, and he obtained forgiveness for his sins, and as it were with a key opened the gates of paradise. By his example I cherish no small hope that by Christ's mercy my sins will be forgiven me. I lack hands and feet, with which I might have the strength to build again what I have destroyed (for all I have left are the lips around my teeth): but he shall receive the calves of our lips [Hosea cap. 14.2], who is merciful beyond belief. Thus with this hope in mind it is my pleasure to offer this calf, to sacrifice this small part of my body and my life.

I confess especially my ingratitude to almighty God; I acknowledge myself most unworthy of all kindness and goodness, but rather deserving of every not merely human and temporal, but divine and eternal punishment, because I committed a most grave offence against Henry VIII and especially against his wife, Queen Catherine, by coming forward as the cause and originator of their divorce; which fault was in truth the seed-bed of all the woes and disasters of this realm. It was from this that arose the murder of so many upright men, from this the schism which split the whole kingdom, from this the heresies, from this the slaughter of so many minds and bodies, such that my reason can hardly grasp. But although these are grave enough and the beginning of woes, I confess I created a huge opening for all heresies, in which I played the part of chief teacher and leader. This, however, especially grievously torments my mind, that I heaped so many blasphemies and insults on the most holy sacrament of the Eucharist, denying that Christ's body and blood are truly and actually contained under the species of bread and wine, even publishing pamphlets in which I did my best to attack the truth, in this respect being not only worse than Saul and the robber, but the most wicked of all the earth has ever borne.

Lord, I have sinned against heaven and before thee: against heaven, which because of me is short of so many inhabitants, because I was shameless enough to deny this kindness which has been shown to us; and I have also sinned against the land, which has been for so long in sore want of this sacrament, against the people whom I held back from this supersubstantial food, being a slayer of so many persons who have perished of hunger. I have cheated the souls of the departed of this regular and eminent sacrament. From all these acts it is plain how also after Christ I maltreated his vicar; I even published books to deprive him of his power. Therefore I mightily and importunately beseech the highest pontiff to pardon me for the sake of Christ's clemency for the offences which I committed against him and his apostolic seat. And I most humbly beseech their most serene highnesses, Philip and Mary of England, Spain, etc. to be so good as to forgive me by the royal clemency which is their special talent. I also beg and beseech the whole kingdom, or rather the whole church, to take pity on this miserable soul, who has now nothing left but his tongue, with which to heal the injuries and damage he has inflicted.

Chiefly, however, since it is against thee alone that I have sinned, I beg thee, most merciful Father (who both desirest and commandest all however wicked to come to thee) to deign to look closely and hard at me, as thou didst gaze upon Magdalene and Peter; or at least as looking from the cross upon the robber, thou didst deign to console his fearful and trembling heart, so too with thy customary and inborn goodness thou mayest turn pitying eyes upon me, and find me worthy to be addressed by thee, saying I am thy salvation, and upon the day of my death, to-day shalt thou be with me in paradise.

This was written in this year of the Lord, 1555 [1555/6], the 18th of the month of March, by me
THOMAS CRANMER
Latin text in *Cranmer II*, pp. 564-5.

Extract 12

And now, forasmuch as I am come to the last end of my life, whereupon hangeth all my life past, and all my life to come, either to live with my Master Christ for ever in joy, or else to be in pain for ever with wicked devils in hell, and I see before mine eyes presently either heaven, ready to receive me, or else hell ready to swallow me up: I shall therefore declare unto you my very faith how I believe, without any colour or dissimulation; for now is no time to dissemble, whatsoever I have said or written in time past.

First, I believe in God the Father Almighty, maker of heaven and earth, etc. And I believe every article of the catholic faith, every word and sentence taught by our Saviour Jesus Christ, his apostles and prophets, in the New and Old Testament.

And now I come to the great thing, which so much troubleth my conscience, more than any thing that ever I did or said in my whole life, and that is the setting abroad of writing contrary to the truth; which now here I renounce and refuse, as things written with my hand, contrary to the truth which I thought in my heart, and written for fear of death, and to save my life if it might be; and that is, all such bills and papers which I have written or signed with my hand since my degradation; wherein I have written many things untrue. And forasmuch as my hand offended, writing contrary to my heart, my hand shall first be punished there-for; for, may I come to the fire, it shall be first burned.

And as for the pope, I refuse him, as Christ's enemy, and antichrist, with all his false doctrine.

And as for the sacrament, I believe as I have taught in my book against the bishop of Winchester, the which my book teacheth so true a doctrine of the sacrament, that it shall stand at the last day before the judgement of God, where the papistical doctrine contrary thereto shall be ashamed to show her face.

A&M, vol.VIII, p.88.

9

'In the clutches of Clio the Muse': Cranmer in Myth and History

Ever since his primacy, Cranmer has been judged a most controversial figure; in consequence he has received a very mixed press. In the words of Professor David Loades (*The Oxford Martyrs*), 'Controversy over the final moments of Cranmer's life began almost before the fire which burned him was cold.' But it was not merely the humiliating episode of the recantations that obliged men to take sides. At the outset, for example, there was what many deemed Cranmer's devious approach to the oath of canonical obedience due to the pope before his elevation to the primacy. As Henry Hallam chose to express it (in the *Constitutional History of England*, 1827):

> ... already a rebel from that dominion in his heart, [Cranmer] had recourse to the disingenuous shift of a protest, before his consecration, that 'he did not intend to restrain himself thereby from any thing to which he was bound by his duty to God or the King, or from taking part in any reformation of the English church which he might judge to be required.

There followed other lapses from what Hallam with hindsight termed 'integrity'. The wretched Cranmer is alleged to have followed a 'discreditable course of temporizing', milestones along which included his role in the 'pretended divorce of Henry the Eighth' (Nicolas Harpsfield); his attitude to Lambert and his seeming lack of consistency over the doctrine of the Eucharist (Lambert was burnt for heresy in 1538), and a general subservience in Court life, whether to sovereigns or protectors, that sounded tones of discord rather than of the high principle to be expected of the kingdom's foremost prelate.

The Cranmer of myth and history can be seen from a glance at the following extracts. First, an exaggerated 'doubting Thomas', the Cranmer of Catholic perspective, a pathetic figure whose political ambition obliged him to yield to Henry's every whim, and whose theological confusion brought about irregular changes in doctrine akin to heresy. This Cranmer is seen as bringing about secular and spiritual scandal, and as a married priest he could not for one moment be allowed to avoid the condemnation of canon law.

The reader can gain some idea of Cranmer in Catholic perspective from the following Extracts:

Extract 1

On 12 September 1555, in the Church of St Mary the Virgin, Oxford, Cranmer was examined before the bishop of Gloucester, James Brokes, papal sub-delegate to Cardinal Puteo for the trial. The proceedings were held on scaffolding in the east end of the university church, the solemnity of the occasion being emphasised by symbolism that placed the presiding bishop under the sacrament reserved at the high altar. Every attempt was made by Dr Thomas Martin, Commissioner to the Crown, to humiliate the archbishop.

Martin: Master Cranmer, ye have told here a long glorious tale, pretending some matter of conscience in appearance, but in verity you have no conscience at all. You say that you have sworn once to king Henry the eighth against the pope's jurisdiction, and therefore you may never foreswear the same; and so ye make a great matter of conscience in the breach of the said oath. . . . Did you never swear obedience to the see of Rome?

Cranmer: Indeed I did once swear to the same. . . .

Martin: Hearken, good people, what this man saith. He made a protestation one day to keep never a whit of that which he would swear the next day. . . .

Martin: . . . ye say you have God's word with you, yea, and all the doctors. I would here ask but one question of you, whether God's word be contrary to itself, and whether the doctors teach doctrine contrary to themselves, or no? For you, master Cranmer, have taught in this high sacrament of the altar three contrary doctrines, and yet you pretended in every one *verbum Domini*.

Cranmer: Nay, I taught but two contrary doctrines in the same.

Cranmer II, pp. 215-18.

Extract 2

Concerning the Archbishop of Canterbury, as he was much worse than the Cardinal [Wolsey], so had he a worse end. He was a scholar and student in the University of Cambridge; and there, being cast in love with a wanton maid at the sign of the Dolphin, that was wont to sell young scholars their breakfasts, married her. It chanced not long after that she died, and then became he a priest...

...Doctor Warham being dead, [Henry] bestowed upon [Cranmer] the archbishopric of Canterbury. Then loe had Cranmer the sweet soppe he looked for, that made him so drunk that he wist not nor cared what he did so he might serve the king's pleasure and appetite....

...This pernicious pestilent prelate, as in Cambridge he began with the flesh, so afterward also (being once inured) he still smelt of the smock. And I have already told you how he carried about with him (like a worthy Archbishop) his darling in a chest...

...he was the first of all Bishops of Canterbury, and of all Bishops in England before our time, that either gave such a filthy precedent and example or sowed such pestilent doctrine.

Nicolas Harpsfield, *Treatise touching the pretended divorce of Henry the Eighth*, edited by N. Pocock for the Camden Society (1878) pp. 289-91

Extract 3

...as Henry had not yet withdrawn from the communion of the Holy See, Cranmer must obtain from the Pope the confirmation of his dignity. He saw at once that every avenue to his consecration was closed against him if he did not declare upon oath, according to the canons, that he would never depart from the communion of the Roman chair; but he saw also into the intentions of the King, who would reject that communion utterly rather than not be married to Anne Boleyn. Under these circumstances the wily man would try by the most profound hypocrisy to serve two masters issuing contradictory commands...

...In the hope of saving his life, he pretended to be a Catholic, and signed his recantations seventeen times with his own hand. In the end his hypocrisy was discovered, and certain bishops having degraded him from all ecclesiastical rank, delivered him up to the secular arm, when he was burnt in Oxford by order of the queen.

Nicolas Sanders, *Rise and Growth of the Anglican Schism*, 1576, edited by David Lewis (1877) pp. 88, 222

Extract 4

His patience in the torment, his courage in dying, if it had been taken either for the glory of God, the wealth of his country, or the testimony of truth, as it was for a pernicious error, and subversion of true religion, I would worthily have commended the example, and matched it with the fame of any Father of ancient time.

'The Testimony of an Adversary', in Strype, *Memorials*, p. 389; quoted in A.F. Pollard, *Thomas Cranmer* (London, 1905), p. 303)

Extract 5

[Cranmer] was a notorious perjured, and often relapsed *Apostata*, recanting, swearing and forswearing at every turn.

William, Cardinal Allen, *A True, Sincere and Modest Defence of English Catholioues that Suffer for their Faith* . . . (1584))

Extract 6

The Tractarians of nineteenth-century Oxford maligned the English reformers even more than had the Catholics, and it is no wonder that Professor Owen Chadwick writes (in *The Victorian Church*, Vol. I, p. 173) that Hurrell Froude's *Remains*, as the 'private journal of a penitent . . . would have been better burnt'. It was, of course, the peculiar nastiness of R.H. Froude that adjudged the 'only good thing about Cranmer' to be 'that he burnt well'. To Froude, 'The Reformation was a limb badly set - it must be broken again in order to be righted.' In his 'Letters to Friends', January 1835, there is also this damning extract: ' . . . why do you praise Ridley? Do you know sufficient good about him to counterbalance the fact that he was an associate of Cranmer . . . ?'

R.H. Froude, *Remains*, 1838, Vol. I, pp. 393-4)

Secondly, there is, of course, the Cranmer of the Protestant cause, a figure accorded paeons of praise for the scriptural commitment of a pastoral ministry that, by preaching the gospel of Christ crucified in terms of justification by faith *alone*, also effectively transformed the Roman Mass into a reformed communion of all the people. Some may still have reservations about the role of the archbishop at the Tudor Court, but the 'Protestant' Cranmer is no longer depicted as a politcal chameleon, but rather as one who did his best in trying circumstances to uphold the doctrine of the 'godly prince' set forth by the apostle Paul. Above all, in the half-light that can at times obscure clear motive, this Cranmer is seen as a principled papist who had about him much of the idealism of a Martin Luther as he strove to achieve genuine reform of the English Church. Opposing rigidity in the canon law, the 'Protestant' Cranmer earnestly studied holy scripture and the Fathers and found there a vision of the primitive Church long denied to the faithful by the superstitions and top-heavy institutionalism of the papal establishment. Cranmer may have recanted, but his final recantation - not to mention the inquisitorial severity used by Spanish friars against an elderly English clergyman - merited both forgiveness and respect.

The following Extracts give the reader insight into the Cranmer of Protestant perspective:

Extract 7

And when the wood was kindled, and the fire began to burn near him, stretching out his arm, he put his right hand into the flame, which he had held so steadfast and immoveable (saving that once with the same hand he wiped his face), that all men might see his hand burned before his body was touched. His body did so abide the burning of the flame with such constancy and steadfastness, that standing always in one place without moving his body, he seemed to move no more than the stake to which he was bound; his eyes were lifted up into heaven, and oftentimes he repeated 'his unworthy right hand', so long as his voice would suffer him; and using often the words of Stephen, 'Lord Jesus, receive my spirit,' in the greatness of the flame he gave up the ghost. ... So good was the Lord both to his church, in fortifying the same with the testimony and blood of such a martyr; and so good also to the man with this cross of tribulation, to purge his offences in this world, not only of his recantation, but also for his standing against John Lambert and master Allen, or if there were any other, with whose burning and blood his hands had been before any thing polluted. But especially he had to rejoice, that dying in such a cause, he was to be numbered among Christ's martyrs, much more worthy the name of St Thomas of Canterbury, than he whom the pope falsely before did canonize.
A & M, Vol. VIII, p. 90

Extract 8

I pray that in this general confusion and overthrow the Lord may afford some aid and assistance to wretched England ... For good men, and, what is yet more distressing, those who take the lead in learning and authority, by whose counsels and prudence many and important measures have been effected in the church, are not only brought in danger of their lives, but are actually under condemnation, and are daily expecting a death, which though desirable to themselves, will yet be lamentable and disastrous to the church. These ought by their example and constancy not only to give encouragement to those of the present age, but to afford an eminent example to future generations. Among whom, Cranmer, Ridley, and Latimer, the bishops of Canterbury, London and formerly of Worcester, having firmly and boldly persevered in the christian doctrine they had embraced, and not allowing themselves to be led away from it by the terror of punishment, death, and the flames, are now condemned, and degraded, as they call it; and are either, I understand, burned [Ridley and Latimer went to the fire on 16 October 1555], or are shortly to experience the power of the flames and the cruelty of their tyrants. It is most painful and distressing to us to be deprived of those, whom, if God should be pleased to effect any alteration of affairs in our wretched and now greatly ruined England, we should not be able, or at least should hardly to able, to dispense with

Sir John Cheke to John Calvin from Strasbourg, 20 October 1555; in *Original Letters*, Vol. I, p. 143)

Extract 9

When constant Cranmer lost his life,
And held his hand unto the fier;
When streames of teares for him were rife,
And yet did misse their iust desire;
When popish power put him to death,
We wishte for our Elizabeth.

'March, 1556', from Thomas Bryce, *The Regester* (1559))

Extract 10

'Hoc fuit tam sancti doctique patris gloriosum martyrium; cuis tota vita divinis vigilis lucubrationibusque transacta ipsis flammis ad coelestem immortalitatem translata est.'

With such conviction, Matthew Parker praised his predecessor in the see of Canterbury. If his work largely edited the assessments of others, and expressed the hope that he would be the last of the English archbishops - 'the number of seventy is so complete a number as it is a great pity there should be one more' - Parker would not look 'to Augustine, Dunstan, Elphege, Anselm, Becket, Edmund, et reliqua pontificia turba' but to Cranmer, who is seen by him to enoble the see of Canterbury in the cause of Christ against the Anti-Christ by the sadness that incredibly brought him to the fire.

De Antiquitate Britannicae Ecclesiae (1572).

Extract 11

His body was not carried to the grave in state, nor buried, as many of his predecessors were, in his own Cathedral Church, nor enclosed in a monument of marble or touchstone. Nor had he any inscription to set forth his praises to posterity: no shrine to be visited by devout pilgrims, as his predecessors St Dunstan, and St Thomas had . . . the rewards of God's elect are not temporal, but eternal. And Cranmer's martyrdom is his monument, and his name will outlast an epitaph, or a shrine . . .

Not contented with the shedding of his blood, unless they stignatized his name and memory, and formed the world into a belief, that he was one of the vilest wretches that lived, who in reality and truth, appeareth to have been one of the holiest bishops, and one of the best men that age produced.

John Strype, *Memorials of Thomas Cranmer* (1694), pp. 391, 467.

Extract 12

All who met at last in final constancy manifested not equal intermediate cheerfulness. Some were more stout, bold, and resolute; others more faint, fearful, and timorous. Of the latter was archbishop Cranmer, who first subscribed a recantation, but afterwards recanted his subscription, and valiantly burnt at the stake. Thus he that stumbleth, and doth not fall down, gaineth ground thereby, as this good man's slip mended his pace to his martyrdom.

Thomas Fuller, *Church History of Britain* (1655-6).

Extract 13

Cranmer

Outstretching flameward his upbraided hand
(O God of mercy, may no earthly Seat
Of judgment such presumptuous doom repeat!)
Amid the shuddering throng doth Cranmer stand;
Firm as the stake to which with iron band
His frame is tied; firm from the naked feet
To the bare head. The victory is complete;
The shrouded Body to the Soul's command

Answers with more than Indian fortitude,
Through all her nerves with finer sense endued
Till breath departs in blissful aspiration:
Then, 'mid the ghastly ruins of the fire,
Behold the unalterable heart entire,
Emblem of faith untouched, miraculous attestation!
Wordsworth, *Ecclesiastical Sonnets [xxxv]*, (1822)

Fortunately, there is also a third tribunal. For through the centuries the historical discipline itself has increasingly challenged both the sensationalism and the sectarianism of Catholic and Protestant judgement. In his *Constitutional History of England*, Hallam did much to set a new style, just as in a *magnum opus* of 1854 a Roman Catholic, John Lingard, began to draw the dragon's teeth. Not that controversy about Cranmer will ever cease, for historians have a duty to stir up the dialectic that is the very nature of their discipline. Like Lord Macaulay, some do so in the grand manner, whilst others, of whom R.W. Dixon provides a good example, can use the critical faculty to temper commitment. Professor Owen Chadwick (in *The Victorian Church*, Vol. II, p. 166) has described Dixon's work as 'the standard Tractarian history of the English Reformation'; the good canon Dixon was arguably as good a disciple of Clio as of the Oxford Movement.

In his inaugural lecture as Regius Professor of Modern History, Dom David Knowles declared before the University of Cambridge that a man's attitude to the martyrs of the Church is inevitably coloured by his decision about the reason for their death. A further comment of Knowles is also relevant: 'Who would dare to say that he could approach the study of Cranmer's life without prejudice or, having approached it, that he had presented Cranmer's actions in their true light?' (*The Historian and Character*, Cambridge, 1955, p. 9).

Nowadays historians need to view the Tudor archbishop against the Renaissance background that, placing the spotlight on the Christian humanism of the great Erasmus, led a cautious scholar to embrace 'the new divinity' before commitment to the cause that was 'the new religion'. In short, Thomas Cranmer was a man of his own times; and however much those of his own, and later, generations, as either determined detractors or fulsome admirers, try to have the last word, history will continue to qualify the archbishop's achievement and keep him partly in sunshine and partly in shade, like the Cambridge man who, but for the *haut politique* of Tudor dynasticism, would never have strayed far from his College down Jesus Lane.

The following Extracts provide sample judgements made about Cranmer in less partisan times:

Extract 14

Few men, about whose conduct there is so little room for controversy upon facts, have been represented in more opposite lights. We know the favouring colours of protestant writers: but turn to the bitter invective of Bossuet, and the patriarch of our reformed church stands forth as the most abandoned of time-serving hypocrites. No political factions affect the impartiality of men's judgement so grossly, or so permanently as religious heats.... If, casting away all prejudice . . . we weigh the character of this prelate in an equal balance, he will appear far indeed removed from the turpitude imputed to him by his enemies, yet not entitled to any extraordinary veneration. . . .

Cranmer's abilities were not perhaps of a high order, or at least they were unsuited to public affairs; but his principal defect was in that firmness by which men of more ordinary talents may ensure respect. Nothing could be weaker than his conduct in the usurpation of lady Jane, which he might better have boldly sustained, like Ridley, as a step necessary for the conservation of protestantism, than given into against his conscience, overpowered by the importunities of a misguided boy. Had the malignity of his enemies been directed rather against his reputation than his life, had the reluctant apostate been permitted to survive his shame, a prisoner in the Tower, it must have seemed a more arduous task to defend the memory of Cranmer, but his fame has brightened in the fire that consumed him.

Henry Hallam, *Constitutional History of England* (1827), Vol. I, pp. 105-6, 107.

Extract 15

When the fire was kindled, to the surprise of the spectators, he thrust his hand into the flame, exclaiming, 'This hath offended'. His sufferings were short; the flames rapidly ascended above his head, and he expired in a few moments. The Catholics consoled their disappointment by invectives against his insincerity and falsehood; the Protestants defended his memory by maintaining that his constancy at the stake had atoned for his apostasy in the prison.

John Lingard, *History of England* (1854).

Extract 16

He was at once a divine and a courtier. In his character of divine he was perfectly ready to go as far in the ways of change as any Swiss or Scottish Reformer. In his charater of courtier he was desirous to preserve that organisation which had, during many ages, admirably served the purposes of the Bishops of Rome, and might be expected now to serve equally well the purposes of the English Kings and of their ministers. His temper and his understanding eminently fitted him to act as mediator. Saintly in his professions, unscrupulous in his dealings, zealous for nothing, bold in speculation, a coward and a timeserver in action, a placable enemy and a lukewarm friend, he was in every way qualified to arrange the terms of the coalition between the religious and the worldly enemies of Popery.

Macaulay, *History of England* (1849 f.) edited by C.H. Firth in six vols. (London, 1913), Vol. I, p. 44.

Extract 17

He died with extraordinary fortitude.... Cranmer was courageous in his timidity, and timid in his courage. His last actions were sublime, but in doing them he was homely. He had no design of majesty and show, when he used that gesture in which his countrymen will ever see him; and the moment before he stretched his hand into the flame he had been searching his breast to find an humble answer to a Spanish friar. If his enemies had avoided the charge of murder, which lies against them, by sparing his life, it is probable that they would have given him the opportunity of earning a clear title to martyrdom. The conjecture of some historians that he would have lingered in remorse, tamely aching to death of a broken heart, is paradoxical. It is more likely that he would have dared the authorities in some open manner, and died in defence of his opinions. The services which this prelate rendered to the Church of England might be measured by the praises of her sons no less than by the maledictions of her enemies, if her sons were unanimous in praises. But some of the keenest of the arrows have been shot by some of those who are not low in the roll of Anglican worthies ... His merits and services were greater than his faults. He had gravity, gentleness and innocency: boundless industry and carefulness: considerable power of forecast: and he lived in a high region. He preserved the continuity of the Church of England. He gave to the English Reformation largeness and capacity. In the weakness which he himself admitted he was servile to many influences: he turned himself many ways in the waters, and allowed himself to be carried very far: but this was not altogether to the hurt of posterity. He was a greater man than any of his contemporaries.

R.W. Dixon, *History of the Church of England* (1892), Vol. IV, pp. 545, 551-2.

Extract 18

There was ambiguity in Cranmer, and something of this has remained in the Church of England ever since.

Edward Carpenter, *Cantuar* (London, 1971), p. 142.

Select Bibliography

Recommended books in print:

Dickens, A.G., *The English Reformation*, 2nd edition (London, 1989). This is *The English Reformation* (first published in 1964) genuinely revised - a brilliant update of a fine original, and in terms of English Reformation Studies *sine qua non*.

Dowling, Maria, *Humanism in the Age of Henry VIII* (Beckenham, 1986).

Elton, G.R., *Policy and Police: The Enforcement of the Reformation in the Age of Thomas Cromwell* (Cambridge, 1977).

Reform and Reformation (London, 1977). The author's second Tudor textbook, and a masterly achievement in historical scholarship.

Fox, Alistair, *Thomas More* (Oxford, 1982). A fine study in intellectual history marking a new departure; this is surely *Encomium Moriae* contemporary style?

Fox, Alistair, and Guy, John, *Reassessing the Henrician Age: Humanism, Politics and Reform, 1500-1550* (Oxford, 1986). An impressive collection of ideological insights.

Guy, J.A., *The Public Career of Sir Thomas More* (Brighton, 1980).

Tudor England (Oxford, 1988). A fine new textbook brim-full of distilled wisdom.

Ives, Eric, *Anne Boleyn* (Oxford, 1986). An immensely readable, yet most scholarly, biography.

King, John N., *English Reformation Literature: the Tudor Origins of the Protestant Tradition* (Princeton, 1982). The first truly comprehensive analysis of English reformation literature.

Loades, D.M., *The Oxford Martyrs* (London, 1970).

The Reign of Mary Tudor: Politics, Government and Religion in England, 1553-1558 (London, 1979).

Ridley, Jasper, *Thomas Cranmer* (Oxford, 1962). A comprehensive biography somewhat marred by a larger-than-period image of the 'Doubting Thomas' in Cranmer.

Scarisbrick, J. J., *Henry VIII* (London, 1968). This is, without doubt, the most distinguished life of 'bluff King Hal'.

Surtz, Edward, and Murphy, Virginia (ed.), *The Divorce Tracts of Henry VIII* (Angers: *Moreana*, 1988).

Williams, Neville, *Henry VIII and his Court* (London, 1971).

Select Bibliography

Articles

Chadwick, Henry, 'Royal ecclesiastical supremacy', in Bradshaw, B., and Duffy, E. (eds.), *Humanism, Reform and the Reformation* (Cambridge, 1989).

Dickens, A.G., 'The Shape of Anti-clericalism and the English Reformation', in Kouri, E.I., and Scott, T., *Politics and Society in Reformation Europe: Essays for Sir Geoffrey Elton* (London, 1987).

Dickens, A.G., 'The Early Expansion of Protestantism in England, 1520-1558', in *A R G*, Vol.78 (1987).

Dowling, Maria, 'Anne Boleyn and Reform', in *J E H*, Vol. 35, No. 1 (January 1984).

Nicholson, Graham, 'The Act of Appeals and the English Reformation', in Cross, C., Loades, D., and Scarisbrick, J. J., *Law and Government under the Tudors: Essays presented to Sir Geoffrey Elton* . . . (Cambridge, 1988).

Slavin, Arthur J., 'Defining the Divorce', in the *Sixteenth Century Journal,* Vol. XX, No.1 (Spring, 1989)

Ullmann, Walter, 'This Realm of England is an Empire', in *J E H*, Vol. 30, No. 2 (April 1979).

Unpublished dissertations

Ayris, Paul, 'Thomas Cranmer's Register' (Cambridge PhD thesis, 1984). This scrupulous study of the archbishop's administration in diocese and province merits early publication.

Nicholson, Graham, 'The Nature and Function of Historical Argument in the Henrician Reformation' (Cambridge PhD thesis, 1977).

Index

Index

Elizabeth, Princess, daughter of Queen Anne, Queen of England (1558-1603), 33, 68

Elton, Sir Geoffrey, 25, 128, 129

Empire, the Holy Roman, 10

Emperor, Holy Roman, *see* Charles V

Enchiridion, see Erasmus

Erasmus, Desiderius, of Rotterdam, viii, 1, 2, 4, 5, 6, 20, 41, 52, 53, 54, 58, 80, 124

Essex, Earl of, *see* Cromwell, Thomas

Eucharist, consecration of the, 6, 56-7, 70, 73; sacrament of the, 27, 54, 57, 59, 66, 67, 82, 91, 112, 114; sacrifice of the, 27, 54, 56, 57, 59, 70, 91, 112

Evensong, service of, 49, 76

Fagius, Paul, 81, 86

Fasting, 46

Fisher, John, Chancellor of Cambridge University, Bishop of Rochester, 1, 28

Flicke, Gerlach, viii

Ford, 35, 36

Fox, Edward, Bishop of Hereford, his role in the King's 'great matter', 8, 18, 19, 20, 21

Fox, Dr Alistair, 3, 25, 128

Foxe, John, the martyrologist, x, 8, 96, 97, 121

Frith, John, 28

Froude, Hurrell, 120

Garcina, Juan de, 95, 98

Gardiner, Stephen, Bishop of Winchester, 19, 26, 32, 33, 42, 56, 67, 69, 70, 78, 80, 89, 91, 92, 116; opposition to Cranmer as Archbishop, 26, 42, 67; controversy with Cranmer on the Eucharist, 69, 78, 116

Gloria, 49, 56, 57

Greek, 5, 6, 47

Greenwich, 8, 32

Grey, Lady Jane, Queen of England, (1556), 90

Greyfriars Chronicle, 57, 60

Grindal, Edmund, 91

Güns-Köszeg, 11

Guy, J. A., 25, 128

Hallam, Henry, 117, 124, 125

Hardenburg, Albert, 82

Harpsfield, Nicholas, 117, 119

Hawkins, Nicholas, 11, 24, 33

Henry II, King of England (1154-89), 38

Henry VIII, King of England (1509-47), 14, 15, 18, 22, 23, 25, 26, 29, 32, 42, 43, 44, 48, 49, 53, 75, 80, 93, 98, 100, 104, 114, 117, 118; his 'divorce' (the 'privy matter'), 8, 9, 10, 11, 12, 17, 19, 22, 24, 99, 114; prefers Cranmer to Canterbury, 11, 16, 22, 23, 31; marriage to Anne Boleyn, 24, 31, 32, 33, 36-8; as Cranmers 'godly prince', 22, 26, 27, 28, 29, 34, 35, 36, 37, 38, 42, 44, 48-9, 75, 80; and the *Bishops' Book*, 28; and the English Bible, 28; and Cromwell's fall from power, 28; and the English Litany (1554), 43, 48, 49, 53; appearance to Cranmer in a dream, 98; vision of 'imperial kingship', vii, 80

Hermann von Wied, Archbishop of Köln, 54, 57, 81

Hertford, Earl of, *see* Seymour, Edward, Duke of Somerset

homilies, 69, 100

Hooper, John, Bishop of Gloucester and Worcester, 56, 67, 69, 72, 84

Hosea, 99, 114

Howard, Thomas, 3rd Duke of Norfolk, 19

Howard, Catharine, Queen of England, (1540-2), 28

Humanism, Christian, 2, 3, 41, 52, 58

'humble access', prayer of, 53, 56, 70

Idolatry, 39, 44, 67, 68, 72

Images, 39, 44

Irenaeus, 74

Ives, Eric, 18, 25, 28, 128

Jerome, St, 53, 105

Jesus Christ, 2, 6, 27, 35, 36, 39, 47, 50, 56, 57, 58, 59, 65, 68, 72, 81, 86, 97, 98, 99, 105, 113, 115; Gospel of, 3, 27, 36, 38, 56, 59, 65, 77, 80, 87, 113

Jewel, John, Bishop of Salisbury, 68

Job, Book of, 37

John, King of England (1199-1216), 38

John Frederick, Elector of Ernestine Saxony, 10, 29, 54

Justification by faith *alone*, 27, 43, 46, 74, 80, 85, 120

Karlstadt, Andreas, 44

Kent, 34, 91

Kings' Book (1543), 42, 44

Kirchenordnung of Köln, (1543), 54, 55

Index

Index